THIS DAY WE
FIGHT!

Tell the problem about God!

THIS DAY WE
FIGHT!

Breaking the Bondage of a Passive Spirit

REVISED AND EXPANDED EDITION

FRANCIS
FRANGIPANE

Chosen
a division of Baker Publishing Group
Grand Rapids, Michigan

Published by Chosen Books
a division of Baker Publishing Group
P.O. Box 6287, Grand Rapids, MI 49516-6287
www.chosenbooks.com

Printed in the United States of America

Library of Congress Cataloging-in-Publication Data
Frangipane, Francis.
    This day we fight! : breaking the bondage of a passive spirit / Francis Frangi-
pane. — Rev. and expanded ed.
        p.   cm.
    ISBN 978-0-8007-9491-0 (pbk.)
    1. Spiritual warfare. I. Title.
BV4509.5.F745 2010
235′.4—dc22   2010000046

Unless otherwise indicated, Scripture is taken from the New American Standard Bible®, Copyright © 1960, 1962, 1963, 1968, 1971, 1972, 1973, 1975, 1977, 1995 by The Lockman Foundation. Used by permission.

Scripture marked MESSAGE is taken from *The Message* by Eugene H. Peterson, copyright © 1993, 1994, 1995, 2000, 2001, 2002. Used by permission of NavPress Publishing Group. All rights reserved.

Scripture marked NIV is taken from the HOLY BIBLE, NEW INTERNATIONAL VERSION®. NIV®. Copyright © 1973, 1978, 1984 by International Bible Society. Used by permission of Zondervan. All rights reserved.

Scripture marked NKJV is taken from the New King James Version. Copyright © 1982 by Thomas Nelson, Inc. Used by permission. All rights reserved.

Scripture marked KJV is taken from the King James Version of the Bible.

15   16   7   6   5   4

Contents

Preface

It is right that we should be aware of end-time events. Indeed, in the last hundred years, a great many prophecies have come to pass. Just as Jesus foretold, "nation will rise against nation and kingdom against kingdom," and we've watched, horrified at the fulfillment of other prophetic events: "In various places there will be famines and earthquakes (Matthew 24:7). We've been amazed at Daniel's predictions for the last days that "knowledge will increase" and "many will go back and forth" (Daniel 12:4). To our dismay, lawlessness has also increased (see Matthew 24:12). To this list, let us not forget the restoration of Israel, a most significant sign of end times (see Ezekiel 36; Isaiah 49).

Yet, while it is clear we live in an era of extraordinary prophetic fulfillment, let us not get ahead of the Lord. Not every prophecy has been fulfilled. We've yet to see the emergence of a central antichrist figure (see 2 Thessalonians 2). There is no worldwide mark of the beast or single international currency (see Revelation 13:17). These things may be close, as it seems the stage is being set, but to be true to the pulse of God, they are yet unfulfilled. In fact, concerning the Antichrist's appearance, Scripture says he will "takes his seat in the temple of God, displaying himself as being God" (2 Thessalonians 2:4). Let us keep in mind that the Temple has not yet been rebuilt. In fact, the Islamic Dome of the Rock and Al-Aqsa Mosque sit on top of the Temple site.

I mention these unfulfilled prophecies so we can rightly calibrate our location on the timeline of end-time events. You see, there is still time to believe God for revival. It is not time to retreat and wait, but time to advance in faith. In fact, Acts 2 tells us that one of the main signs of the last days will be a great, final outpouring of the Holy Spirit upon all flesh. This last great movement will not be a little thing; rather, it will be accompanied by confirming "wonders in the sky above and signs on the earth below" (Acts 2:19). During this last season the Gospel of the Kingdom of Heaven will be proclaimed in all the world for a witness, just as Jesus said, "and then the end will come" (Matthew 24:14).

There are difficult times awaiting planet earth, but also spectacular times of revival and harvest as well (see Isaiah 60:1–3). We will have to fight. Perhaps the most frequently mentioned end-time sign is the spiritual passivity that will lull many to drowsiness and indifference concerning the things of God (see Matthew 25). It is this paralysis of passivity that I hope to expose in this book.

Introduction

Overcomer.

Ultimately, if we intend to follow Christ, we must think of ourselves not just as Christians, but more specifically as overcomers. The Church is overstocked with people who identify themselves as Christians but have no determined will to fight the fight of faith. They simply have adjusted to the level of their oppression and now tolerate a religious, but mostly empty, spiritual life.

Beloved, it is not enough to sit regularly in church or even be familiar with the promises of God. We are called to possess them! The Bible says it is "through faith and patience" that we overcome and gain heaven's treasures (Hebrews 6:12; see also Revelation 2:3). Although some breakthroughs might take years in coming, we must not quit. Christ assures us that our lives can change, and that when they do, we, like salt and light, will transform the world around us.

There may be numerous reasons why so many Christians have attained so few of God's promises. One core reason, however, is they are in bondage to a passive spirit, which is the theme of this book.

Passivity arrests our will in many ways. We may have become lukewarm because we have been disappointed; or perhaps we are harboring offenses and hardening our hearts; or maybe we have been living an undisciplined or sinful life. The source of our spiritual passivity may also be demonic warfare, or it may be fear or just poor health or diet. Yet whatever makes us spiritually passive also leaves us spiritually vulnerable.

Let me explain. The virtue of Christianity does not flow from dogma or church services, although these are vital elements of our faith. Our source of spiritual life flows from our daily union with God in Christ. We do not bear fruit on our own. Jesus said if we abide in Him, then we will bear "much fruit" (John 15:5). He tells us to come to Him when we are "weary and heavy-laden" (Matthew 11:28). Even the Scriptures themselves, though they bear witness to the life of Jesus, cannot produce His life. We must come to Him to have life (see John 5:39–40). Nothing in the doctrine of what we call Christianity can, in and of itself, substitute for the life we draw uniquely from Jesus. We are as strong and invulnerable to spiritual attack as we are close to Him.

Because the enemy knows it is our nearness to God that produces our strength, the first stage of his attack involves a preliminary deception that makes us feel as if we are cut off from Christ. The moment we accept this illusion of detachment, the devil is disarming us.

Yet it takes little more than our passive acceptance to keep us trapped. Passivity does not feel like sin; it does not specifically violate any of the Ten Commandments. Its deception is more like a drug that clouds our discernment. Thus, breaking passivity is often the first stage in breaking deception and seeing our hearts released.

I have written *This Day We Fight!* because I have seen too many Christians who have lost their first love for God. When love grows cold, a door opens in our souls toward darkness. We become vulnerable to other sins. Indeed, Jesus promised that "the one who endures to the end, he will be saved" (Matthew 24:13). Between now and the end of our lives, we will find many obstacles arrayed before us. Each battle comes like a thief to "steal and kill and destroy" (John 10:10). I suggest we examine our lives and take inventory: What have we lost over the years? We may have survived the battles but lost our joy. We may still be attending church, but our vision has grown dim. We may still know God is holy, but our thought-life has become unclean.

We can get our lives back, but we must overcome passivity. We must defeat the illusion that our current condition is our permanent condition.

My prayer is that this book will stimulate your faith once again and that you will be empowered to reengage the battles of life with new zeal and divine wisdom. My hope is not only to expose the nature of a passive, immobilizing spirit, but to inspire us to walk as "more than conquerors through him who loved us" (Romans 8:37, NIV).

PART 1

Fighting the Good Fight

The LORD will go forth like a
  warrior,
He will arouse His zeal like a man
  of war.
He will utter a shout, yes, He will
  raise a war cry.
He will prevail against His enemies.

Isaiah 42:13

1

The Bronze Bow

The Bible not only reveals to us the nature of God, but it also tells the remarkable stories of those who, in their generation, served God. Concerning the lives of these men and women, the writer of Hebrews says:

> And what more shall I say? For time will fail me if I tell of Gideon, Barak, Samson, Jephthah, of David and Samuel and the prophets, who by faith conquered kingdoms, performed acts of righteousness, obtained promises, shut the mouths of lions, quenched the power of fire, escaped the edge of the sword, from weakness were made strong, became mighty in war, put foreign armies to flight.
>
> Hebrews 11:32–34

In many ways and in many places God's Word tells us that, if we will reach true spiritual maturity, we must learn to overcome. I do not mean we will not have peace or rest for our souls, but that along the way we will begin to truly discern the enemy, move in Christ's authority and learn perseverance in the fight of faith.

If we learn our lessons well, we can see the blessing of God restored to our hearts, our families and even to cities and nations. Do not doubt nor tremble, nor excuse yourself as being too weak. Remember what Hebrews 11 says of those who overcame: "from weakness [they] were made strong" and they "became mighty in war" (v. 34).

Let me share with you a little of my story. Although I am not where I will ultimately be in walking out Christ's victory, I am further along than when I first started. Walking in victory, to me, first means I know God's promises in His Word; but second, it means I have been trained to have insight into spiritual warfare. Indeed, it was in the midst of battle that the Lord began to develop my sense of discernment.

Revelation through a Dream

I am sure that at various times in my life, I have prayed, "Lord, whatever You desire for me, I'm willing." At the same time, I have never specifically asked to know about spiritual warfare. Yet needing discernment was exactly where I found myself back in the mid-1980s. I was pastoring a church that included a number of emotionally needy people and was clearly under-equipped to handle the variety of problems we were facing. In fact, this season had become for me a time of weariness and extended warfare. I needed grace to know the nature of the diverse battles I was fighting.

The breakthrough began in a dream one Friday. I found myself in a barren, one-room house; I was exhausted and trying to rest. Suddenly several church members entered, warning me that our spiritual enemies had returned. Once again, I was needed to engage this demonic horde in battle.

I remember lamenting in the dream, *Why am I always called when there is battle?* Tired and weary, I stepped outside. I could see a row of enemy warriors on top of a ridge, sitting on horses and looking down in our direction. Someone nearby handed me a bow and arrows. I shot, but my aim wavered, and my arrows, at that distance, all fell short. My depression deepened as I heard the mockery of the enemy warriors, who scorned my attempts to hurt them.

Suddenly the heavens opened, and an outstretched arm handed me a shining, gold-colored bow. (I wish I could have more of these dreams!) As I grasped it, the Word of the Lord rose immediately within me, and I proclaimed, "By my God I can bend a bow of bronze!" (see Psalm 18:34). Instantly energy surged through my arms, while confidence and courage filled my spirit. I nocked an arrow against the bowstring, aimed and fired toward the opposing warriors.

This time my arrows had distance, penetration and accuracy. The enemy was routed.

The Awareness Grows

That was the dream, and it definitely made an impression. But the Holy Spirit was set on confirming His word to me. Early the next morning, Saturday, I drove to the church to do some work. A letter awaited me. It was sent by a visitor who, after attending our service the previous week, felt compelled to share something the Lord had put on her heart. After words of greeting, she said the following Scripture was for me:

> For who is God, but the LORD?
>   And who is a rock, except our God,
> The God who girds me with strength
>   And makes my way blameless?
> He makes my feet like hinds' feet,
>   And sets me upon my high places.
> He trains my hands for battle,
>   So that my arms can bend a bow of bronze.
>
> Psalm 18:31–34

17

As I read her words, I again felt strength from the Holy Spirit pour like oil upon my head and flow down into me.

There were other confirming witnesses as well, such as the preacher who visited our church the day after I read the letter. Quoting Elisha's word to King Joash, he spoke Sunday night on "the LORD's arrow of victory" (2 Kings 13:17). Between the dream, the letter and the preacher's words, that whole weekend was one of those "God weekends" that launched me into a new level of spiritual warfare.

I do not mean in any way that I never stumbled again or that I now had a graduate degree in spiritual warfare. No, I just began to gain revelatory insight into spiritual realities that had been mostly invisible to me before. A gift of discernment was developing within me, and with it came increased spiritual authority in my ministry.

Over the next months and years, the Holy Spirit began to unmask many covert works of the demonic realm. The Lord also revealed the nature of demonic strongholds—thought systems that must be toppled from people's minds before deliverance can be completely secured. I do not mean to say that I never failed in this anointing. I still had (and have) many flaws. But I now could discern the enemy at work and could take action to thwart his plans. Also, I had greater confidence in personally taking spiritual authority when dealing with the demonic realm.

What made the difference? The Holy Spirit gave me a special grace for battle. He "trained my hands" and gave me weapons. Before this time, I could have given you a fairly accurate theological definition of spiritual warfare. Afterward, I actually had an anointing to wage warfare. During the years that followed, I began to write my second book, *The Three Battlegrounds* (Arrow, 1989), a compilation of truths concerning spiritual warfare and discernment that the Lord revealed to me during this time.

Weapons of War

My quest in this book, *This Day We Fight!*, is to help equip Christians to discern the enemy. I also wish to expose the spiritual paralysis that passivity can cause. With all my heart I believe we can turn back evil in our land. Therefore, let's return to David's words and experiences in Psalm 18, for they give us insight into two important strategies toward these ends.

First, we must allow God to make our way blameless. We will not be successful if we harbor sin. Harboring sin that we have not repented of is like allowing a saboteur to live within our hearts; if we do not confess it, our sin will undermine our spiritual authority. So we must walk humbly and, as much as we can, purely with the Lord.

Second, we cannot fight in our own strength or with human reactions; we must fight in the strength of the Lord. This means we do not run off and attack whatever we find offensive in life. Rather, we follow our King into battle. It is written, "The armies of heaven were following him" (Revelation 19:14, NIV). We must learn how to follow. Religious zeal, by itself, will only burn us out.

As the deer places its rear feet exactly in the imprints of its front feet, so we must learn to put our feet exactly in the steps of the Lord, especially when He sets us "upon . . . high places" (Psalm 18:33). As the Lord "makes [our] way blameless" (verse 32), He trains our hands for battle and gives us supernatural weapons against the enemy.

Not only has God called us to war, but He has also given us powerful spiritual weapons. One of the mightiest weapons in our arsenal is spiritual authority. The devil would like to take this world and spin it completely out of orbit, thrusting it into terrible darkness and chaos. God calls us to resist the devil and use our authority to bind and cancel demonic advances into our world.

There is a difference between prayer and spiritual authority. I believe fully in praying, in asking the Lord to take action against the devil. To plead for divine help is both scriptural and effective. Times do come, however, when the Lord requires us to exercise His authority. In such cases, the Holy Spirit commands us to turn from the act of prayer itself and, in the name of Jesus Christ, confront the demonic power that has come against us.

Instead of functioning in Christ's authority, however, too often we fail to discern and confront our enemies. It is this passive stance that most frequently hinders us from becoming effective in spiritual warfare. I see this as a primary reason for weariness in the Church. Some of us, instead of moving toward victory, settle for temporary relief. We ask God to make the devil leave us alone, while the Lord is telling us to pursue our enemies and scatter them like dust! Our passivity can neutralize the attitude of a warrior. The moment we finally receive a little peace, we begin to beat our swords back into plowshares. God calls us to be prayer warriors, not prayer worriers!

Others of us have been so conditioned by defeat that we are fearful of exercising spiritual authority. We look at Christians moving in authority over the devil as though there were something sinful or doctrinally wrong with them. However,

- Having confidence is not a sin.
- Exercising our faith is not presumption.
- Standing on God's promise when others flee is not foolish.

We must pray with vision, courage and confidence; and with equal confidence we must answer the call when the Lord summons us to stand and face our enemy. We do this by taking up the weapon of spiritual authority.

The Authority of Christ Our King

For God's Kingdom to advance, we must move in the authority of the King: "Your arrows are sharp; the peoples fall under You; Your arrows are in the heart of the King's enemies" (Psalm 45:5).

The Holy Spirit is our bow, and our prayers are God's arrows. Under the Spirit's anointing, they plunge deep into the heart of the Lord's spiritual enemies.

Someone might argue, "God hasn't called me to face principalities and powers."

Fine, but note that I am not talking about foolishly challenging world rulers of darkness. How about confronting that little demon of lust that keeps you shamed and condemned? Do not start by attacking the devil himself, just that spirit of fear that keeps whispering unbelieving thoughts into your mind.

Someone else may say, "But I've failed. I've suffered some very serious setbacks."

So you lost a round or two. Is the whole fight over? Is that a white flag I see in your hand? Have you conceded?

Another might respond, "I don't feel comfortable confronting evil. I just want to hide in God as His worshiper."

No one is saying that you must never hide in God or that you have to stop worshiping. No one is urging you to run into the night and throw hatchets at the moon. But if you are being spiritually harassed even after you have tried to hide in God, maybe the Lord Himself is bumping you out of the nest. Perhaps your victory will not come until you turn and face your spiritual foes in the authority of Christ.

Beloved, we must break free from the stranglehold of passivity. The fact is, if we do not use the authority of Christ daily, then no matter how hard we try to break free, it is likely that we will continue to experience some degree of harassment from the demonic realm. Prayer and repentance are irreplaceable stages of deliverance; they should be part of our spiritual lifestyle. They may not be enough, however, if an unclean spirit is complicating our freedom. We must turn and face our enemy and, in the context of repentance, command that spirit to depart.

The Lord can, of course, utterly vanquish the devil, and He can do so in a heartbeat—sometimes He does just that! But there are also times when it pleases Him more to "crush Satan under your feet" (Romans 16:20).

Remember, I am not saying that we should all focus on the devil. I am saying this: Let's focus on the anointing God has given us to stand against the schemes of the wicked one! Let's reintegrate divine authority into our prayers and spiritual warfare, taking up the "full armor of God" (Ephesians 6:11).

As we do so, we become equipped to use the most powerful weapon in the universe—"the sword of the Spirit, which is the word of God" (Ephesians 6:17). The weapons of our warfare are "mighty through God to the pulling down" of Satan's strongholds (2 Corinthians 10:4, KJV). Before David picked up his bow of bronze, he secured himself in the Lord. God became his stronghold, his refuge and high tower.

If you have already found the Lord as your place of safety, then it is time to fight in the strength of God against unrighteousness.

As we pray and enter the fight with the authority given us, let's also receive that anointing of the Lord of hosts that we might, in His strength, bend a bow of bronze against the enemy!

Let's pray this now:

Lord, not only have You called us to war for ourselves and our loved ones, but You have also given us weapons that are mighty. Father, I bring everyone who has become spiritually timid or intimidated by the enemy before You right now. I ask You to stir them from their fears and, through Your Holy Spirit, anoint them for this day of battle. Grant us all grace, blessed King, to receive from Your hand a bow of bronze. In Jesus' name, Amen.

2

Fighting the Fight of Faith

The Spirit of God does not want us merely to tolerate oppression; He desires us to conquer it. He has not called us to passivity; He has called us to fight the fight of faith! God has anointed us with the power of His Holy Spirit, and Jesus has given us His authority over all the power of the enemy (see Luke 10:19). This authority of the Lord is not just for guard duty or defensive maneuvers. The Holy Spirit desires that, as we follow Christ, we take the battle to the enemy as well.

When David sings in Psalm 18 that, under God's anointing, he can "bend a bow of bronze," he also states: "I pursued my enemies and overtook them, and I did not turn back until they were consumed" (verse 37). Let's make this clear: David was first a worshiper of God. He did not pursue his enemies without first pursuing God. But when the Lord led him into war, he *thoroughly* defeated his foes.

I will tell you a solemn truth: *Either we pursue our enemies or our enemies will pursue us.* We must develop Christ's attitude toward evil. He came "to destroy the works of the devil" (1 John 3:8). The Bible says, "Hate evil, you who love the Lord" (Psalm 97:10).

The Holy Spirit is looking for determination in us so that, like David, we will pursue our enemies until they are consumed. It is, in fact, this aggressive attitude of heart that causes us to grow into mature Christlikeness. Jesus could live with and forgive human failure, but He never allowed evil spirits to control Him. He was aggressive toward His spiritual enemies. There is no neutral ground. There is no room for a passive spirit in God's army.

Attack and Counterattack

Let's take a classic example of our need to act aggressively against our enemy: the battle for the mind. We touched on the idea of deliverance in the last chapter. If you are frustrated repeatedly by fear, self-pity, anger, immoral thoughts or fleshly lusts, you know that these ideas and feelings will not go away by themselves. Your mind must be renewed through repentance and the knowledge of God's Word. And if there is demonic activity exploiting your sin nature, that enemy must be confronted in the authority of Jesus' name. Whether you are fighting fear, lust, anger or any other sin with its corresponding demonic strongman, you are in a war for your soul.

Some people respond to this by saying: "I don't have a problem with an evil spirit; my battle is with sin." And I agree. Frequent failure in a particular area might genuinely be rooted in the carnal attitudes of our old nature. But if you have repented repeatedly and still cannot find lasting freedom, perhaps the issue is a combination of sin and the devil's manipulation of that sin. The real power behind recurring failure may well be demonic.

25

Now suppose you address that demonic power and use your authority to free yourself from the evil spirit. Is that the end of your struggle with that particular sin and the accompanying demonic hold? No, it is not. Even if you embrace true repentance and find functional spiritual freedom from demonic oppression, the enemy will try to reenter your life. Recall Jesus' warning: "Now when the unclean spirit goes out of a man, it passes through waterless places seeking rest, and does not find it. Then it says, 'I will return to my house from which I came'" (Matthew 12:43–44).

Jesus explains that even if you have had a genuine deliverance by the hand of God, a time may still come when that "unclean spirit" seeks to return to the "house from which" it came. The "house" it seeks to reenter is its former dwelling, which was created in your soul by your carnal thought-life. The way it seeks access is to masquerade as your own thoughts. Jesus warns that if the unclean spirit returns and finds your soul unguarded, it comes with "seven other spirits more wicked than itself" (Matthew 12:45).

Do you see the progression of this counterattack? First, the enemy will infiltrate your mind, seeking to plant a thought or sow an idea in your soul. Then he will attempt to water that seed with corresponding temptation.

In the battle for the mind, we must capture those initial, invasive thoughts. We must be vigilant to recognize and conquer the oppression before it leads us back into sin. As soon as we discern the ungodliness of a thought, we can turn and take authority over it. We must not let it multiply. We must not let it dwell for even a moment. If we fail to use our authority, though, if we sit down inside and allow that seed to grow, the enemy will then attempt a full-scale invasion. Jesus says that "the last state of that man becomes worse than the first" (Matthew 12:45).

Do you see that we must be aggressive in our prayers and actions? Satan will attack and counterattack. To win, in the midst of everything else we do, we must guard our hearts and minds. To do this we must exercise spiritual authority aggressively.

Present Attitudes and Future Victories

An Old Testament story captures well my concern with the effects of a passive spirit. Elisha the prophet was about to die, and Joash, king of Israel, in an unusual show of affection, wept over the man of God. Adding to the intrigue, the king then spoke the very words that Elisha had himself uttered to Elijah in the last hours of his mentor's life: "My father, my father, the chariots of Israel and its horsemen!" (2 Kings 13:14).

It is possible that the king sought from the prophet some special blessing for victory in battle. Elisha did accommodate the king, yet he also tested him. Ordering the king to take a bow and arrows, Elisha told him, "Put your hand on the bow." Elisha then laid his hands on top of the king's hands and said, "Open the window toward the east." Joash opened it. Elisha said, "Shoot!" And as Joash shot, Elisha proclaimed, "The LORD's arrow of victory, even the arrow of victory over Aram; for you will defeat the Arameans at Aphek until you have destroyed them" (2 Kings 13:16–17).

God thereby declared through Elisha that He was going to honor King Joash for recognizing the anointing on this prophet and seeking his blessing. Yet one test remained. Elisha told the king to take the arrows and "strike the ground." Joash took the arrows, but he struck the ground only three times and stopped. At this the prophet became angry with him and said, "You should have struck five or six times, then you would

27

have struck Aram until you would have destroyed it. But now you shall strike Aram only three times" (2 Kings 13:18–19).

Elisha was angered by the passive spirit in King Joash. He saw that the king did not possess the perseverance to pursue his enemies until he fully conquered them.

What does this mean for us? The prophet's anger actually mirrors the Lord's displeasure toward the passiveness or laziness of His people today. Is it hard to believe that Jesus would actually be angry with His Church? Then consider the Lord's word to the church in Laodicea, a church that was overly concerned with its own comfort and passive in its attitude toward spiritual realities. Jesus said, "I know your deeds, that you are neither cold nor hot; I wish that you were cold or hot. So because you are lukewarm, and neither hot nor cold, I will spit you out of My mouth" (Revelation 3:15–16).

Jesus would rather we were hot or cold than lukewarm. Does He still love those He rebukes? Of course, but He calls us to change our attitudes. It is not that passivity or laziness is such terrible sin, like murder or adultery. It is simply that such attitudes create a psychological prison around believers that actually holds us hostage to our other sins.

The Lord is not pleased with the spiritual passivity and indifference so prevalent among His people. We are aware daily that terrorists could attack with massive destruction; we watch the advance of perversion in our cultures—yet many Christians remain prayerless and inactive. This is in spite of the Lord's promise that if we will come before Him, humbling ourselves in earnest prayer, He will empower us to pursue our enemies and defeat them. But instead of seeking God's face on behalf of the lost, too many of us are immobilized by the grip of a passive spirit.

I am not talking about the level of energy in our bodies, but about the level of fire in our obedience. Elisha could see that King Joash was a quitter by the passive way he struck with the arrows.

Beloved, God has given us authority and He has given us the weapons of our warfare to help us, but we need to get up and fight. We need to repent of a passive spirit and stand with Christ's authority in this day of war and battle. For if we fail to do either—pray or act—we might actually lose the soul of our nation. Our defeat might come not because God's help was not available, but because we saw the advance of evil and did nothing.

For maximum benefit, pray this prayer *out loud*:

> *Lord God, I thank You that You have given me authority over all the power of the enemy. Forgive me for allowing my voice to remain silent and my will to remain immobilized by a passive spirit. I realize that to be an overcomer I must pursue my enemy until he is consumed. You have given me authority over the plans and works of evil. You have created me to be a minister of Your righteousness. You have filled me with Your Holy Spirit and with fire. This day I confront, renounce and take authority over the power of the enemy. I break the bondage of a passive spirit. In Jesus' name, Amen.*

3

This Day We Fight!

We are in the midst of one of the most important and difficult conflicts since World War II, yet too many Christians are sitting idle on the sidelines. The passive spirit has attached itself to the soul of multitudes in the Church. It is a subtle malaise that has settled like a blanket upon the devotional life of many.

Yes, they remain heartsick about the escalating lawlessness in the world, but their voice of intercession has quietly diminished. Many Christians in my country, for example, feel outraged that activist judges are usurping our legal system, but how quickly we adjust to injustice as our outrage fades into a shrug of the shoulders and a sigh.

We have discussed receiving the Lord's anointing and authority for spiritual warfare, and King David has served as an example to follow. Let's turn now to a story from his life that is quite different—a time when a passive spirit immobilized his will.

The Effects of a Passive Spirit

Scripture contains many examples of David's valor. As a young man, for instance, while others trembled, David was ready and eager to face Goliath. David is an example of one whom God chose, whose passions for God sustained him for most of his life.

Yet David also provides an example for us of what happens to good people when a passive spirit triumphs. For there was an occasion when David did *not* pursue his enemies, and the consequences were grave. It happened because he allowed a passive spirit to subdue his will.

> Then it happened in the spring, at the time when kings go out to battle, that David sent Joab and his servants with him and all Israel, and they destroyed the sons of Ammon and besieged Rabbah. But David stayed at Jerusalem.
>
> 2 Samuel 11:1

During a time of war, the king accepted a passive spirit into his soul. Soon we find this great warrior king almost helpless to resist the unfolding spiritual attack.

> Now when evening came David arose from his bed and walked around on the roof of the king's house, and from the roof he saw a woman bathing; and the woman was very beautiful in appearance.
>
> 2 Samuel 11:2

The woman was Bathsheba, the wife of Uriah. From the moment David accepted the influence of that passive spirit, his resistance was weakened. A paralysis of conscience occurred. Scripture says that "when evening came David arose from his bed." Perhaps it was customary to rest in the afternoon, but it strikes me as inconsistent for David to nap while his men fought. It is possible that this nap was not a response to a bodily need, but an expression of the slumber that gripped his soul. He was in bed until "evening."

This heaviness of soul resting on David was actually part of a larger, synchronized spiritual attack. The other part of that battle was the quiet, inner prompting that stirred Bathsheba to bathe in a place where David could see her. Finally, David, unable to resist and in defiance of his noble qualities, "sent messengers and took her, and when she came to him, he lay with her" (2 Samuel 11:4).

Dear friend, remember: This terrible moral failure was not driven by David's lust or flagrant rebellion to God. *A passive spirit introduced David to his sin!* The problem was simply that, in a time when the kings went forth to war, David stayed at home.

We ourselves are in a time of war. The Spirit of God is calling us to fight for our souls as well as for our families, cities and nations. Indeed, God's Word reveals that "The LORD will go forth like a warrior, He will arouse His zeal like a man of war. He will utter a shout, yes, He will raise a war cry. He will prevail against His enemies" (Isaiah 42:13).

Is that holy fight in you? Is there a war cry in your spirit? If you are born again, that cry is within you, even if it has been muted by lethargy. *lack of interest*

We will never succeed as overcomers without carrying in our spirits the war cry of God. We must stop resisting the call to prayer; we must embrace the reality of spiritual warfare; and we must fight with the weapons of warfare that God has given us, both for our own progress and also on behalf of those we love.

Conversely, the moment you surrender your will to a passive attitude, you should anticipate that a temptation appropriate to your weakness will soon follow. It may not be Bathsheba; it may be pornography on the Internet. Or it may be a co-worker who begins to look attractive at a time when you and your spouse are struggling. Whatever the area of weakness in your life, Satan will seek to exploit that area. Remember, the enemy's first line of attack likely will not be bold and obvious. He will first work to disarm you with a passive spirit. If the enemy succeeds in his assault, you will find yourself wrapped up in something that can devastate you and your loved ones.

World and National Conflicts

Just as we must guard our souls vigilantly, so we must persevere also in prayer before God for our world. Indeed, God's Word says that His house shall be called a "house of prayer for all nations" (Isaiah 56:7, NIV; Mark 11:17, NIV). The Lord has predetermined that He Himself will intervene in shaping reality according to the influence of those who pray. In other words, the future is not only determined on the battlefield, but also in the prayer room. When we pray for the nations, God bends reality and moves life in the direction of redemption; when we fail to pray, life descends into deeper chaos.

Consider our conflict with radical Islam. Spearheading Muslim radicalism is the ideology of jihad, a central Islamic doctrine. While most Muslims interpret jihad as a personal war to win their souls, terrorist organizations like Al-Qaeda and many others see jihad as a command from Mohammed—something to be fulfilled by his faithful against the non-Muslim world. Radicals know that if the West were to surrender or quietly withdraw from pursuing terrorists, the radicals would soon wrest control over nations that possess nuclear capabilities. Nations such as Pakistan that already have nuclear weapons would be able to spread nuclear terrorism around the world.

I know we do not want to think about these things, yet we cannot be passive about our prayer. We need divine intervention. Our intelligence-gathering networks, our soldiers, our diplomats all need the Holy Spirit's help. Even more, we do not simply want an end to war, we need to pray as Jesus commanded us—that God's Kingdom would emerge in Muslim nations in power, in healing, in the revelation of Jesus Christ to multitudes, including those in government positions and especially those who are currently radicalized terrorists.

We also need to lift up our eyes above the headlines of our news agencies and see the Islamic world as Christ sees it—ripe for the harvest. Therefore, we must "beseech the Lord of the harvest to send out laborers into His harvest" (Luke 10:2). This is a clear, essential command: We are to pray for God to raise up and send forth laborers into the ripening nations.

Some may argue, asking if these Muslim countries really are ripe for harvest. Already millions of Muslims have been born again and have found faith in Christ. We cannot be conditioned by unbelief or fear; we must know the Word of God and believe it! Jesus said, "This gospel of the kingdom shall be preached in the whole world as a testimony to all the nations, and then the end will come" (Matthew 24:14). "All the world" includes that part which, today, is currently Islamic. Muslims will encounter a time when the love and power of Jesus Christ will be revealed to them. Of course, not everyone will be saved, but multitudes will come to Christ during the days ahead. There will be a witness of the Kingdom of heaven (not necessarily of traditional Christianity, which many Muslims see as corrupt). The Holy Spirit will be poured out on all flesh (see Acts 2), and we can expect healing and power such as we see in the book of Acts to happen in Tehran, Gaza, Kabul and many other places. The frontier of our warfare is not political, but spiritual. Our victory is measured in the advancing of God's Kingdom, and in this we have a definitive role to play in God's will.

Yet, while Islamic terrorists plot to infiltrate and conquer the non-Muslim world, many other demonic conflicts are advancing within our own culture. There exists an unprecedented breakdown of the family; permissiveness and perversion are rampant. Government and big business have become increasingly corrupt. No wonder Muslims are fighting to remove Western influences!

We are at war. The very fabric of our culture is being attacked from within, and Christians, whom Jesus called salt and light, are sitting passively in darkness, unresponsive. What can we do? We can join school boards, form action committees, write letters to the editor, join other Christians to protest, support godly elected leaders, organize church groups, write congressmen, run for political office, pray, prayer walk and do spiritual warfare. We can take a stand against unrighteousness.

Do you see the striking parallels between our world and King David's situation? We are in a season of life when kings are going out to battle. In the context of that battle, where are we? If we are not out fighting on some level, if we are only sighing from heaviness, dear friend, our world is in trouble indeed. This is a day when kings go to war, not a time when we can comfortably nap away our responsibilities.

The Fight before Us

The conflict we face with Islam is no less threatening than Nazism or Soviet Imperialism. Radical Islam is a demonic power that seeks world domination. We cannot lose the war against terrorism. Nor can we sit idly by while perversion infiltrates our communities—or abortions take millions of lives or godless secularism fills our government or the stranglehold of poverty continues to exist. We must not allow fear

35

or unbelief into our hearts and minds, for we were born to fight and win the battles of our times.

This argument often arises: "I was taught that there isn't much point in fighting for our culture because life is only going to grow more evil until Christ returns."

Yes, such a day of final darkness will come, but we must not assume that it has arrived. The spread of wickedness must be confronted by the power of the Holy Spirit in the Church. Regardless of the size of the battle before us, no matter how dark the spiritual atmosphere becomes, we must stand and fight for the purposes of God in the earth.

You are no doubt familiar with the Lord of the Rings trilogy written by J. R. R. Tolkien and made into popular movies. Tolkien, an Englishman, always denied that his work had anything to do with the realities of World War II. Yet much of his manuscript was written during the height of that time, when entire civilizations were at war. He was clearly influenced by his time. In any event, the book is a metaphor for all times and conflicts, especially highlighting the role of common men to attain uncommon levels of valor and victory against forces of evil.

In a scene from the third Lord of the Rings movie, *The Return of the King*, Aragorn seeks to inspire his hopelessly outnumbered men against what seems like sure defeat: Hell's swarming legions have amassed before them, and the courage of Aragorn's fighters is weakening.

Riding along the front lines of his gathered but rather lowly army, he shouts:

> I see in your eyes the same fear that would take the heart of me. A day may come when the courage of men fails, when we forsake our friends and break all bonds of fellowship. But it is not this day. . . . This day we fight! By all that you hold dear on this good earth, I bid you stand, men of the West!

Let's also put aside our fears and the burdens of a passive spirit. Let's take up the sword of the Spirit, which is the Word of God. And let's war on behalf of righteousness. A day may come when the world will succumb to the forces of evil. But it is not this day. This day we fight!

Lord Jesus, gird me with courage for this hour. Equip me with vision and faith. Teach me how to stand and persevere in the battle, even as You protect our land from our enemies. Be with our armies and let them serve Your holy purposes. In Jesus' name, Amen!

4

The War Mode

I was seventeen years old, a senior in high school, and was slouching into my desk when an angry student easily twice my size entered the room. Suddenly he saw me. In a storm of spit and fire, he burst toward where I was sitting, grabbed me by my neck and began rearranging my facial features.

I learned later that a prankster had written a derogatory remark about him on the inside cover of his notebook and signed my name to it. Obviously, there was more going on in the Big Guy's life than anyone was aware of. Whatever other frustrations had been accumulating in his heart, his immediate goal was to release his fury on the latest offender, whom he considered to be me.

I should also mention that at the time I was five foot nine and weighed 135 pounds. So it was logical that instinct taught me to "turn the other cheek" in times of conflict. Granted, the turning of my cheek was not born of character but of cowardice. My quest for peace with potential enemies was the result of my fear of being hurt. I had, in fact, developed several clever ways of avoiding confrontation while still appearing relatively cool among my friends.

It does not matter, however, what one's philosophy is concerning conflict when one is actually *in* a fight with an angry giant. Big Guy was not looking to talk; he was looking for blood. The sole awareness flooding my mind was that he was not going to stop. If this assault was going to end, it would be because I put my whole heart into fighting back.

Once I accepted that I was in a fight, something amazing happened inside me. Instead of my fear getting worse, it actually left. The energy that had been expended through terror was suddenly recycled and enlisted for my defense.

At that moment, unexpectedly, I discovered another dimension of my soul: *the war mode.*

Frankly, I did not even know I had a war mode, but when Big Guy reached down to pick me up for "round two," my fight instincts clicked into action. It had been easy for him to throw me around when I was not resisting, but now I sprang upward with a punch that landed squarely on his nose. He fell back a step. I hit him again two or three times and then jumped on him while he was off balance, knocking him to the floor. I admit it is possible, on reflection, that he stumbled over a chair and my punch had nothing to do with his fall, but it did not matter. When his back hit the floor, there was a 135-pound Sicilian on top of him.

By now, students were pulling *me* off of *him*. Blood was pouring from his nose, and his friends were calling me a bully. When the teacher entered the room, it plainly looked as though I was the aggressor and Big Guy was the victim, cowering beneath my relentless assault. I nearly failed to graduate because of the incident, but I did not care. Something inside me had changed. I had found the war mode. I still did not go around looking for a fight, but I was not afraid of one either.

Passivity Is Not Peace

Why am I telling you this story? First of all, it is not because I think physical violence is the answer to our problems. I tell it to emphasize the fact that a "war mode" exists in each one of us, and it is time to recognize and appropriate it—not in a physical sense, unless you are a soldier in service to your country, but in a spiritual sense as a soldier in God's army. We are at war on a global scale, and physical war always calls Christians to spiritual war. This aggressive stance is governed by love for people, but it is fearless and uncompromising against the powers of darkness.

We must not confuse false peace, which is the result of compromise because of fear, with real peace, which comes from faith in God to help us in our war against evil.

Today many are weary with world events. Part of this weariness is because hearts are divided: We are trying to maintain a peacetime mentality during a time of war. Since 9/11 our souls have secretly longed to return to 9/10. Yet we cannot hide in the past. As long as we are on earth, we have a role to play as Christians. We must pray for our leaders, support our troops and intercede for mercy to fall upon the Muslim people. We must engage in the intercessions of Christ. And we must follow through fearlessly in spiritual warfare, praying aggressively against terrorism and the demons that drive terrorists to fulfill evil.

Governments Administer Justice

The argument rises that it is wrong for a predominantly Christian nation to go to war. The objectors point, of course, to Jesus as their model. Would Jesus go to war?

That question is only part of the equation. Christ set the pattern not for governments, but for His disciples. As His disciple, I follow Him in the way of mercy and redemption. God's command to governments, however, is different from His word to disciples. Part of the role of government is to administer justice and to exercise punishment.

Some may argue that this is Old Testament thinking, but the New Testament is clear on this subject as well. Speaking in reference to governing (or civil) authorities, Paul writes that a secular government, to the degree that it executes its courts fairly, serves as "a minister of God." Paul warns: "If you do what is evil, be afraid; for [a government] does not bear the sword for nothing; for it is a minister of God, an avenger who brings wrath on the one who practices evil" (Romans 13:4).

Because I follow Jesus Christ, the Lamb of God, my job is to exhibit Christ's love and mercy, not to be "an avenger who brings wrath." A national government, though, in re-spect to the exercise of punishment against evil, serves as "a minister of God" when it brings wrath upon the "one who practices evil." The individual who says that governments of "Christian" nations should turn the other cheek—that they should not punish evil or that the wicked should be free to fulfill evil without consequence—is denouncing justice. This leads to anarchy.

God calls governments to fulfill His standard of justice, and He requires the Church to reveal His standard of mercy. Both unveil aspects of the nature and will of God.

The Spiritual Side of War

In the grand scheme of things, the Bible tells us there is a legitimate "time for war" (Ecclesiastes 3:8). But whether you agree that this is such a time is not what is most important; it is always legitimately the time for prayer. We must not surrender our prayer. God can still work a miracle of redemption over the Middle East.

The sooner we switch into war mode, the faster we will tap into the moral resolve needed to defeat personal oppression and enter the spiritual side of warfare. As we do so, self-pity and passivity will diminish, and we will find God's grace to prevail.

Beloved, it is conceivable that more major terrorist attacks will occur, either in the United States or in other allied nations. I am not resigned to this possibility; I am praying aggressively against it. But if it happens and I am knocked down by the suddenness of the assault, I will stand back up quickly. I will rise with the attitude of one who has entered the war mode.

Will you join me?

Master, I submit to Your anointing for warfare. I renounce being a coward or embracing a false peace based on compromise. I submit to the fighter in You, who can sanctify the fighter in me. In Jesus' name, Amen.

5

Love-Motivated Warfare

If we succeed in these difficult days, it will be, in part, because we have renounced the seductive limitations that accompany a peacetime mentality. Indeed, we must embrace an aspect of spirituality that is unfamiliar to many Christians—one that is both militant and vigilant toward evil, yet compelled by the purity and fire of Christ's love.

The Holy Spirit has been calling the Church to rise in intercessory prayer and to exercise spiritual authority. With holy urgency in my heart, I say we do not have time to languish in self-pity about life's injustices. In a time of war, we must not be distracted by inconveniences or grievances. We must possess a war mentality. The good news is that hell would not be in such a frenzy if heaven were not advancing. God is working to bring revival and spiritual awakening to our nations.

Thus, while we face concern about the advance of evil, we can be encouraged that many among the people of God are meeting evil with resistance. The enemy's multifaceted attacks will be repulsed and even reversed as we stand and fight. My immediate appeal is for us to war in prayer, with passion and confidence. Remember, as the Church of Jesus Christ, we are not fighting against flesh and blood but against principalities and powers and the world rulers of darkness (see Ephesians 6:12). These ruling spirits hold influence over every nation and culture on earth; we must all be involved. Whatever efforts we make in the natural realm, our focus and victory originate from the spiritual realm: Things visible come from things invisible (see Hebrews 11:3). So we must war in prayer, using the Word of God as our primary weapon and the blood of Christ as our primary defense.

A True Peacemaker

I often hear the argument: "Our nation may be in a war, but I am a peacemaker like Jesus. The Lord has not called me to war."

I, too, am a peacemaker. At the core of my quest for Christlikeness is the ministry of reconciliation and peacemaking. Scripture says that "the seed whose fruit is righteousness is sown in peace by those who make peace" (James 3:18). This means we must never forget that our message is the Gospel of peace. At the same time, it is the "God of peace" who has chosen to "crush Satan under [our] feet" (Romans 16:20). Peace has a militant side: True peace manifests because we have confronted and overcome our spiritual enemies.

The problem is that too many Christians have confused peace with passivity. They have hollow peace instead of hallowed peace. Their lives are prayerless, and they live in perpetual compromise with heaven's enemies. This is not peace; it is bondage. Jesus was the quintessential peacemaker, yet He boldly confronted the advance of evil. And He did so with unbending righteousness and unsheathed spiritual authority. Christ *terrified* the demonic realm. At His approach, evil spirits howled in trembling dread: "Have You come here to torment us before the time?" (Matthew 8:29). Jesus was operating in the war mode, and they knew it.

Not only did Jesus exercise authority over every demonic hierarchical strata up to Satan himself, but He told the disciples that the works He did, including those of spiritual warfare, they would also do (see John 14:12). The disciples were trained to function in the war mode: They learned discernment, understood authority and usually engaged in the fight of deliverance with perseverance. Jesus specifically gave them authority "over all the power of the enemy" (see Matthew 10:1; Mark 3:14–15; 6:13; 16:17; Luke 9:1; 10:17–19), and He assured them that "nothing [would] injure" them (Luke 10:19). Of course, He taught them to walk in purity and built into their souls certain fundamental safeguards. Yet after preparing and commissioning His disciples with His authority, He ministered faith to them, not fear.

When I read the Scriptures, it is plain to me that Jesus was always operating in a mode of *spiritual aggression* toward the powers of hell. He was perfectly God-focused, but His radar was continuously sensing the enemy's advance into His world. When Peter sought to dissuade Jesus from accepting the cross, Jesus discerned in Peter's words the voice of Satan. Speaking directly to the spirit manipulating Peter, Jesus rebuked the prince of devils, driving him from the thought-life of the apostle. When Jesus sent out the seventy disciples, they went forth in a war mode. When they returned from their mission, they marveled that even demons were subject to them in Christ's name (see Luke 10:1–20). Jesus commanded His disciples to follow Him into heaven's battles.

45

I know we picture Jesus as eternally kind and unfathomably gentle, and such He was with the victims of life's injustices. (His compassion was also an act of war against evil.) Yet the disciple who wrote that God is love and whose ear listened to Christ's very heartbeat also said that the Son of God came "to destroy the works of the devil" (1 John 3:8).

Do we see this about Christ? Jesus came not only to restore and redeem a fallen world but also to "destroy the works of the devil." As a follower of Christ, have you destroyed anything evil lately? Have you toppled any demonic strongholds this week? Have you rescued anyone imprisoned in sin or fear or demonic captivity? Evil can be destroyed in a hundred different ways, not merely in a "deliverance" session. The sad truth is, historically, too many of us have neither a plan nor a prayer to see evil truly destroyed.

We need to have an "attitude" toward evil. Imagine if, in addition to fulfilling our other spiritual disciplines and virtues, every Christian began truly to pray with the authority of Jesus Christ. Without exaggerating the role of the devil, consider the heavenly impact praying Christians would have if we all renounced passivity, unbelief and fear. Paul said the weapons of our warfare are mighty. Imagine if we actually used them!

Life in a War Zone

Planet earth is not a place of peace but a realm at war. From the casting out of Lucifer and his angels from heaven, to the temptation in the Garden of Eden, to Babylon and the multiplication of nations under satanic influence, ours has been an embattled world. The idea that somehow our era is less threatened by evil is the height of deception. We must fight if we will follow Christ into victory.

No matter how beautiful the world around us seems, remember there was a serpent lurking in Paradise itself. If Adam and Eve had possessed a war mode mentality, they never would have accepted the lies of Lucifer so casually. Likewise today, we need to be wise and walk carefully, for "the days are evil" (Ephesians 5:16). Jesus was always aware that He lived in a war zone. No matter what He was doing—whether He was laughing with sinners or driving out demons, whether He was healing the sick or training followers—beneath the surface of His outer activities, the "war mode switch" in Jesus' mind was always on.

A word here to women who find warfare a solely macho topic. I have heard a few women argue, "I'm just a housewife, a mom. I don't have a war mode." If your child were seriously sick, would you not fight that illness with everything at your disposal? You would fast and pray, and you would do so from your war mode. If your marriage were under spiritual attack, would you not get before God and war with fervency? The fact is, you know how to fight. Ask your husband if he thinks you have a war mode. You just need something to wake it up, because once you begin to shift into the war gear, in the Holy Spirit you are dangerous!

The war mode is in us all. It may be attached to our instinct for survival, but it is more directly connected with our love for people. I love my nation, so I am warring in prayer on its behalf. Because of love for my family, I war in prayer on their behalf. I love my church, my city and, yes, even my own soul, so I war to protect what I love. If there is a natural fight instinct, there is a spiritual fight mode as well. It just needs to be awakened, submitted to Christ and then unleashed against the enemy. If you have a love mode, you also have a war mode. God has created the war mode so we can protect the people we love.

Lord, I repent for not loving people enough to fight for their well-being. Master, You fought for us and for love gave Your all. I pattern my life after Yours. Let my warfare be an expression of my love, both for You and for my loved ones. In Jesus' name, Amen.

6

Embracing the Fight of Faith

In spite of worldwide conflicts, the Holy Spirit is guiding the true Church into her greatest season of transformation. We must not look at the pressures of our times as though they were obstacles set to restrict us. For in the hands of the Almighty, these are the very tools He is using to perfect us.

One of the problems of interpreting end-time events is the tendency to focus upon only one set of conditions. If we look only at the fact that Satan is raging or that lawlessness, wars, earthquakes and famines are escalating, we might conclude that difficulty and darkness are all that we have awaiting us until the Rapture. And, as I mentioned, many people have been taught that life will only grow more evil until Christ returns.

But the same Spirit who predicted the perilous conditions at the end of the age also forecasts that, in spite of difficulties and battle, the Gospel of Christ's love will be proclaimed worldwide to all nations (see Matthew 24:14). The Lord also said that the "crop" of last-days Christians will reach full stature (see Mark 4:28–29), and that those who know their God will be strong, do exploits, shine like the stars and lead multitudes to righteousness (see Daniel 11:32; 12:3).

In every age God requires that we walk as overcomers. Our call is to pray, to stand in spiritual warfare, to intercede for our leaders and soldiers and not to surrender our vision of a world in revival, regardless of whatever temporary setbacks we may face. The very fact that some distant nations are experiencing renewal and great harvests in recent years (Uganda and Fiji, for instance) reminds us that there is still time for our own nations. Our focus must remain riveted on becoming like Christ in all things.

We might feel overwhelmed by the flood of evil storming against our societies, yet the promise of God is that, when the enemy comes in like a flood, He shall raise a standard against him (see Isaiah 59:19, KJV).

So we must ask ourselves, is our focus on the enemy's flood? Or are we aware of the standard God is raising up to counter the onslaught of evil? Do not forget, beloved, that even when darkness covers the earth and deep darkness the peoples, the promise of God is that His glory shall rise upon us and His presence shall be visibly seen through us! In spite of the appearance that darkness is never ending, the Lord promises that, at the end of the war between light and darkness, "nations will come to your light, and kings to the brightness of your rising" (see Isaiah 60:1–3). Indeed, God's Word reveals that nestled and unfolding in the panorama of end-time events will also be an ongoing "period of restoration" (see Acts 3:20–21).

This does not mean that the world will be subdued by the Church (as some erroneously teach), but that the true Church itself will be glorious, subdued and transformed by Christ! This final display of grace will be consummated in a Christlike

Church, whose spiritual maturity shall manifest on earth the person and passions of Jesus Christ Himself.

Our fight is the fight of faith: *Do we believe what God has promised?* Our war is against principalities and powers: *Do we believe the report that Christ shall "sprinkle [that is, cleanse, and bring forgiveness and transformation to] many nations" (Isaiah 52:15)?*

I, for one, believe the promises of God. His Word is not just a comfort to me in times of trouble but a sword that I wield in times of spiritual war. His faithful Word is what I proclaim over my family, my church, my city and nation! Consider His proclamation: "So will My word be which goes forth from My mouth; it will not return to Me empty, without accomplishing what I desire, and without succeeding in the matter for which I sent it" (Isaiah 55:11). No matter how the battle rages, God's Word shall not return to Him void.

Consider also His commitment: "I am watching over My word to perform it" (Jeremiah 1:12). And His accessibility:

> "Do not say in your heart, 'Who will ascend into heaven?' (that is, to bring Christ down), or 'Who will descend into the abyss?' (that is, to bring Christ up from the dead)." But what does it say? "The word is near you, in your mouth and in your heart"—that is, the word of faith which we are preaching.
>
> Romans 10:6–8

We are not mere mortals stumbling blindly on earth, separated from God and isolated from His response to our needs. No! We are new creatures, born again from above, and resident within us is the Holy Spirit of Almighty God.

Yes, we labor and intercede; we repent for our sins and the sins of our nations. But the weight of our victory rests not on how much we labor and groan, but on how sincerely we believe what God has promised. The Lord does not want us worrying about the future; He wants us to *create it* through the knowledge of His will, through the proclamation of His Word—which is the "sword of the Spirit" (Ephesians 6:17)—and through our yieldedness to the power of the Holy Spirit. And then He promises, "Whoever believes in [Me] will not be disappointed" (Romans 10:11).

Beloved, the sword God has put in our hearts and mouths is nothing less than the echo of His voice in us! So, let's not whine about negative conditions in the world or sigh prayers muttered in fear and unbelief. Let's embrace the fight of faith! May Christ's love for mankind be our compelling motivation! Pick up your Bible and speak audibly the promises of God's Word. Pick any verse quoted above and speak it out loud, with faith and authority. I guarantee that if you proclaim God's Word with faith, it will release power in and through your spirit. No power can quench the promises God has inspired in His Book.

He assures us, "All things are possible to him who believes" (Mark 9:23). Let's break the bondage of a passive spirit. Let's take up the sword of the Spirit and embrace the fight of faith!

Lord, I repent of self-pity and fear. Train my hands for war! Teach me to stand and fight back on behalf of Your righteous cause. In Jesus' name, Amen.

PART 2

Exposing the Enemy's Weapons

Now these are the nations which
the LORD left, to test Israel by them
(that is, all who had not experienced
any of the wars of Canaan; only in
order that the generations of the
sons of Israel might be taught war,
those who had not experienced it
formerly).

Judges 3:1–2

7

Overcoming Discouragement

An Old Testament story reveals the effect of discouragement and how it can immobilize and render passive even righteous people with a vision from God. Because of the Israelites' long and extended rebellion against God, He had allowed Nebuchadnezzar to defeat them and take them as captives to Babylon. In the hard years of their exile, the Lord did not leave them without encouragement. He spoke these words through the prophet Jeremiah: "After seventy years . . . I will visit you, and perform my good word toward you, in causing you to return to this place" (Jeremiah 29:10, KJV). The seventy years had finally passed, and the Israelites' season of hardship was over. It was time for the Lord's promise of restoration to be fulfilled.

Israel entered a season of divine visitation initiated by the fasting and prayer of the prophet Daniel. The Lord personally revealed Himself to King Cyrus of Persia, a Gentile king, and "appointed [him] to build [the Lord] a house in Jerusalem" (2 Chronicles 36:23). King Cyrus responded by encouraging a national offering for Israel's journey, restoring the treasures taken by Nebuchadnezzar from Israel and issuing a royal edict authorizing the return of the Jews to the Holy Land. Israelites with integrity and vision were raised up as leaders to undertake this great work.

The display of divine grace created an atmosphere of excitement and even awe among the people of God—*the Lord Himself was "causing [them] to return" to Israel!*

It was a season of great grace, supernatural provision and fulfilled prophecy. Yet even as the exiles resettled in Jerusalem and engaged in the hard work of restoration aided by God Himself, something happened that stalled their progress. We read that they allowed themselves to be diverted: "Then the people of the land discouraged the people of Judah, and frightened them from building, and hired counselors against them to frustrate their counsel all the days of Cyrus king of Persia, even until the reign of Darius king of Persia" (Ezra 4:4–5).

Incredibly, in spite of the miracles, signs and provisions, simple *discouragement* neutralized the progress of God's people. Scholars say that their work of restoration stalled for nearly twenty years!

Beloved, discouragement is an enemy that is both subtle in its attack and powerful in its ability to paralyze our progress. When discouragement approaches our hearts, we must discern it. We must refuse to accommodate its influence when it speaks.

Like the returning Israelites, you and I may have a true vision from God—a mission or a blessing that He has for us as we grow strong in our spiritual authority. Indeed, just as Israel was given a promise from God and provisions to make it happen, so the Almighty has given promises and provisions to us. The vision may be for personal transformation; it may be a God-inspired desire to see our families or churches brought into spiritual renewal. We may even possess a citywide vision or a holy passion to see our nation turned toward God. Yet before that vision comes to pass, we can be assured that we will face serious opportunities to become discouraged. Like the Jews, we can be just as vulnerable to discouragement and its effects. Just as it stopped them, so it can stop us if we are not walking in faith.

Building a Fighting Spirit

I know that many Christians want to pray and fight, but they feel that oppression hangs on them. You may be one of them. Isaiah 61:3 KJV talks about "the spirit of heaviness." The NASB renders this "a spirit of fainting." Whether we call this evil a spirit of heaviness, fainting or passivity, it is what keeps people from exercising their spiritual strengths. Indeed, it often sits on the upper chest, seeking to smother our spiritual energy and godly heart initiatives.

This spirit gains access to our lives through a number of means. Disappointment with loved ones will open us to this spirit. Or it might infiltrate our souls if we repeatedly sin in a particular area. It is also a companion to condemnation and fear. Whatever the door, if this has entered your life, you need to repent of any active sin in your life and then renounce it forcefully and vocally. Forgive any people you need to forgive and release all areas of disappointment or discouragement that may have come from your personal failures. Renounce living with condemnation and fear. Since God gives you the garment of praise for the spirit of heaviness, recall the many blessings of God in your life. Put on that garment of praise and spend a few minutes praising and thanking God for His goodness in your life.

You might pray something like this:

In Jesus' name, I submit to God, my heavenly Father, and I command this spirit of heaviness and passivity to depart from me. I also pray for it to leave my loved ones and any members of my church it has targeted as well.

This is not a time to pray quietly. Pray aggressively and with your eyes open. Incidentally, I hear people say that they cannot pray with their eyes open, but that is not true. People often pray with their eyes open while driving.

The point is that this passive spirit seeks to trap you inside yourself. This is why it is important not to whimper out a quiet, eyes-closed prayer. Speak loudly. Look up to God and pray with faith and spiritual authority. Even if you feel like a phony, as if you do not truly mean what you are saying, say it anyway until the spell of passivity is broken over you. The sense of being artificial will fade as you regain access to your true spiritual self. You will soon find meaning once again in spiritual words and prayers. *Praise God!*

The Need for Courage

Everything God tells us to do will, at some point, require us to stand against seemingly impossible odds and believe courageously what He has said. Here is a principle that I will repeat in subsequent chapters: *True faith takes courage.* When Jesus healed people, He often told them to "take courage." Not only was Christ offering courage to the downtrodden, but He was also offering courage to help them focus their faith on the God-potential that was at hand. Thus, in the midst of human struggle, courage must walk as the companion and expression of our faith.

This is why the Church desperately needs encouragers. The book of Acts tells of a certain disciple, a Levite named Joseph, who was also called Barnabas by the apostles. *Barnabas* means "son of encouragement." This man's ministry was encouragement. His calling was to instill courage in the hearts of the early saints. When Mark deserted the apostles, Barnabas desired to take the young disciple (who was also his cousin) under his tutelage and give him another chance. Paul resisted Barnabas's decision to the degree that a division arose between them. Yet because Barnabas did not give up on this young man, in time God used Mark to write and proclaim the Gospel.

As for Paul, at the end of his life when many had deserted him, he asked for Mark. Because of the encouragement of Barnabas, Mark was now a mature, committed man of God useful to Paul in those latter years (see 2 Timothy 4:9–11).

In the conclusion to the above story of the Israelites' return to the Holy Land, we learn that their vision was finally fulfilled when the prophets encouraged Israel's elders in the work of rebuilding (see Ezra 5:1–2).

Discouragement is the opposite of encouragement. To be encouraged is to have courage imparted to us; to be discouraged is to have courage removed. Faith without courage will always falter.

How Discouragement Enters

How does discouragement gain access to our souls? We become discouraged whenever we start evaluating our negative circumstances based upon information supplied by our senses. The antidote, therefore, is to form our opinion of life based on the promises and goodness of God.

This does not mean we become oblivious to our problems or the negative situations we may be fighting. It does mean that in spite of circumstances, we stand and put our faith in God. Consider: When God promised Abraham and Sarah a child in their old age, the Bible says that Abraham "contemplated his own body, now as good as dead since he was about a hundred years old, and the deadness of Sarah's womb" (Romans 4:19). Abraham did not deny his bleak circumstances. Without growing weak in faith, he "contemplated" the impossibility of his situation from a human perspective. He thought about it deeply.

But he also thought about the greatness, goodness and power of God. He considered his limitations, but he also believed that with God nothing was impossible. Here is what God's Word says about Abraham (and this was something that earned him the title "the friend of God"): "Yet, with respect to the promise of God, he did not waver in unbelief but grew strong in faith, giving glory to God" (Romans 4:20). Abraham was "fully assured that what God had promised, He was able also to perform" (verse 21).

Discouragement comes when we look *only* at our circumstances without looking to the faithfulness and integrity of what God has promised. We grow "strong in faith" each time that, in spite of our circumstances, we give glory to God.

Here is a prayer similar to what I have often prayed when I feel discouraged:

> *Lord, You are great, You are able and You are good! I give glory to You, praising You, trusting You to be my strength and the provider for my life. I believe in You and, according to Your Word, trust that what You have promised You are also able to perform.*

How Courage Comes

As I have walked with God these many years, I have known too many who have fallen prey to discouragement. Perhaps you have fought this battle, too. Jesus knew mankind's vulnerability and taught His disciples a parable to show that "at all times they ought to pray and not to lose heart" (Luke 18:1). The parable concerns a widow who desperately implores a judge to give her legal protection from an adversary, but she receives no immediate help. In spite of the judge's resistance, however, she refuses to be discouraged from her quest; she persists until she gains her breakthrough (see verses 1–8).

The goal of Christ's teaching was to immunize His followers against discouragement. Jesus assures us that God will hear us as we turn to Him in persistent prayer.

We need to remember as well that Christ is not only our Savior but also the "author and perfecter" of our faith (Hebrews 12:2). Faith is not merely a proper understanding of doctrinal issues; faith is the spiritual "substance of things hoped for, the evidence of things not seen" (Hebrews 11:1, KJV). Not only must we possess accurate doctrines *about* faith; the righteous also *live by* faith.

Indeed, in order for faith to mature, it needs situations where faith alone can sustain us. For this reason God will allow us to go through times when we must trust Him in spite of how things appear. In those times, against the glaring face of a negative reality, true faith arises, appropriates courage and locks into the integrity of God's promise. We must let faith arise in the context of resistance. This is the faith that touches God's heart.

The enemy comes to *dis*-courage, or remove the courage from our hearts. This causes us to withdraw into unbelief. To win our fight of faith we must not surrender to discouragement. Yes, times will come when we will need to ask God

61

for greater wisdom; and certainly, we will have to adjust our attitudes and become more flexible and wiser as we process the faith assignment destiny has set before us. But we must not give up: "For yet in a very little while, He who is coming will come, and will not delay. But My righteous one shall live by faith; and if he shrinks back, My soul has no pleasure in him" (Hebrews 10:37–38).

The Hall of Faith

The above verses from Hebrews 10 are actually the introduction to Hebrews 11, which chronicles the heroic stories of those who pleased God with their faith. All of them had to endure the test of time; often the delays must have seemed permanent and the tasks before them insurmountable. Yet all of them were fighters. None of these men and women allowed discouragement to dim the brightness of their faith. The persevering quality of their hearts—the fact that they stood in the storms of doubt and circumstances and refused to shrink away from God's promise—filled God's heart with pleasure. God altered the history of man and changed nations through the power of their faith.

Look at what the Bible says these individuals accomplished:

> [They] conquered kingdoms, performed acts of righteousness, obtained promises, shut the mouths of lions, quenched the power of fire, escaped the edge of the sword, from weakness were made strong, became mighty in war, put foreign armies to flight.
>
> Hebrews 11:33–34

I absolutely love these words of Scripture: They conquered kingdoms and put foreign armies to flight. Beloved, as we look

62

around us, we see that a foreign army, demonic in nature, has invaded our culture. The enemy has come with weapons of perversion, immorality, deception and corruption. The enemy has eroded the conscience of our society, and it seeks to carry off our sons and daughters into captivity. We must fight.

You say, "But Francis, I have so little to encourage me."

Yes, there are times when we all feel the heaviness of the battle. But we have the help of God with us. Consider His promise: "Behold, My Servant, whom I uphold; My chosen one in whom My soul delights. I have put My Spirit upon Him; He will bring forth justice to the nations. . . . He will not be disheartened or crushed" (Isaiah 42:1, 4).

Christ will not be "disheartened or crushed." Why? The Spirit of God "upholds" Him, and the Spirit of God upholds Christ in us as well. Are you God's servant? Then turn to Him and find new strength. You and I may be wounded or stuck, but as we abide in Christ we, too, will be neither disheartened nor crushed.

Dear one, there is a spiritual war raging over the future of our very souls. We cannot shrink back into unbelief. Let's be strong and of good courage. Let's seek God and find new strength in prayer. And let's never give in to the voice of discouragement.

Lord, You were neither disheartened nor crushed as You lived Your life. The Father upheld You in Your mission. I ask You today to uphold me. Grant me new strength, restore my soul and empower me by Your Holy Spirit. For Your glory I pray, Amen!

8

If We Do Not Lose Heart

> He will speak out against the Most High and wear down the saints of the Highest One, and he will intend to make alterations in times and in law; and they will be given into his hand for a time, times, and half a time.
>
> Daniel 7:25

The prophet Daniel warns of a time when Satan, through the Antichrist, will seek to wear down the strength of God's saints. How this occurs in the final hours of the age remains to be seen, but on one level this battle already is going on today: Satan seeks to wear us out through delays ("alterations in times") and in compromise of God's Word ("alterations . . . in law").

The final effect of what seems like never-ending delays is that believers are worn out. Do you know anyone who is weary with his or her battle? Are you yourself weary? I know many who seem trapped in situations that should have been remedied months and even years ago, but the battle continues against them. Situations and people, often empowered by demonic resistance, stand in opposition to the forward progress of God's people. As a result of satanic spiritual resistance, many Christians incrementally accept this resistance until a quiet, but weighty, oppression rests on their souls.

This battle to wear out the saints may be rooted in conflicts with children or spouses; perhaps it is some unresolved issue or division within their churches. It may be a work conflict or health battle, yet on and on it goes. Like a skilled and masterful thief, the enemy daily steals the joy, strength and passion of Christians, and many do not even realize what they have lost or how much.

The scale is actually larger than our personal struggles. Consider the various conflicts in the world. Some have continued for generations. We can understand why, even in the midst of great worship and praise by the redeemed, there is a place under the altar in heaven where the saints continue to ask, "How long, O Lord?" (Revelation 6:10). Fifty-eight times in the Bible, from beginning to end, the phrase *how long* is echoed by those who grew weary with waiting.

On the one hand, sometimes the delays are God-ordained to perfect faith and character. On the other hand, there are also occasions when Satan seeks to resist the fulfillment of God's plans until we grow weary and quit. Satan is the dragon whose goal is to "drag-on" the battle with draining, wearying delays. He persists until we wear out, give up and quit praying.

Additionally, as situations stretch beyond reasonably expected conclusions, weariness of soul can also exacerbate the original situation, leading to fleshly reactions or just overreactions, which also need resolution. We lose patience, eventually seeking relief rather than victory. This compromises the standards of God and conscience.

65

Weariness of the Mind

Have you grown weary? You are not alone. Part of the weariness we feel comes from faulty thinking. If we had known the battle was going to take as long as it has, we would have prepared for it more realistically. Every building plan will probably take twice as long as we assume; every virtue will take a year, not a weekend, to be truly worked in us. It may take a generation for some of our loved ones to be saved. If things happen sooner, we can rejoice. But we must guard ourselves lest we prepare only for the easiest of breakthroughs. Some things will not manifest without time and tears.

When I travel, I pray and trust God for divine help, and often I am rewarded with perfect flights and no delays. Yet I have also learned to accept the fact that I will occasionally arrive later than expected. I am not shocked by flight cancellations; I anticipate them. While others are fretful, I am calmer, trusting God. My peace enhances my witness of Christ when I speak to people standing near me, waiting anxiously.

You may think that it sounds like unbelief to expect difficulties such as delays on flights. I do not think so. I think it is wisdom. Wisdom is not the enemy of faith. I have found that if I do not trust God and relax, I become anxious, fretful and distracted. I have also found that the Holy Spirit will not descend and rest in power upon a man who is fearful and controlled by his external circumstances. Jesus' spirit stayed in abiding peace, yet still He accommodated delays as part of life's package. He was often delayed by the huge crowds or urgent needs of the people around Him. People died waiting for Jesus to show up. Did He become anxious? No, He stayed focused on the Father and, without losing His trust in God, simply raised the dead.

At some point we must come to the conclusion that God knows when we are growing weary in battle—be it praying for the salvation of a loved one or experiencing one more frustrating delay in reaching our vision. We must trust that He knows we are wearied and that He has a miracle conclusion awaiting us. I know a dear pastor who labored long and hard with a new building project, but it was constantly delayed. It was first scheduled for completion in September, then rescheduled for December, then January and then February. Finally, with weariness in his voice, he called and asked if I could join him for their dedication. It was set for the first week of March.

"When exactly do you need me?" I asked.

He answered, "March fourth."

Suddenly the Holy Spirit illuminated my heart. I told him that God had chosen this date prophetically. The Lord wanted that church, as an army, to "march forth" into their destiny. In a flash, the weariness weighing upon him was gone; joy and a sense of destiny swept his soul. The delay wore him out, but the delay in the hands of God became inspirational.

Dear ones, let's persevere. We just do not know what the victory will look like when we finally break through. Consider Joseph. Betrayed, enslaved, slandered and forgotten, he had to endure to reach his destiny. But the time finally arrived, and never in his wildest dreams could he have imagined that the outcome would be so wonderful.

What we *become* is more important to God than what we *do* for Him. Our struggle, though we may have been delayed time and again, deepens our character. Maintaining our standards when pressed, finding grace when stretched, makes us true men and women of God. The Almighty One is in control. He knows how to take what was meant for evil and transform it into something good, even using the devil's own devices to bring him down. God has something marvelous in store for us, otherwise the enemy would not be fighting so intensely. Indeed, Scripture tells us that Satan rages worst when he knows his time is short (see Revelation 12:12).

Character before Breakthrough

We mentioned Daniel earlier as a prophet who warned about Satan's ploy to wear down the saints. God gave him a vision of the end of the age. Here is what he wrote: "I kept looking, and that horn was waging war with the saints and overpowering them" (Daniel 7:21). This is the nature of the battle. There are times we feel war storming against our souls, overpowering us. But the prophet said the sense of overpowering continued only "until the Ancient of Days came and judgment was passed in favor of the saints of the Highest One, and the time arrived when the saints took possession of the kingdom" (Daniel 7:22).

There is a principle here that, once understood, will lead to victory in our battles. Inevitably, a time will come when we feel overpowered. Yet if we endure, if we climb higher into God, if we refuse to lose our trust in God, a time will come when the Ancient of Days enters our circumstances. Looking at our newly developed character, which has grown strong through perseverance, He will pass judgment in favor of our cause. God looks at our character, forged in the fire of overpowering delays and battle, and says, "Good, this is what I was waiting for."

Whatever your battle, whether you are praying for this country or standing for your children, whether your cry is for the lost or for the end of some local or personal conflict, remember the words of Paul: "Let us not lose heart in doing good, for in due time we will reap if we do not grow weary" (Galatians 6:9).

Master, I ask that You work in me the character that perseveres until the end. Forgive me for being such a wimp. Help me to grow up, to stand up until the harvest I have sown spiritually bears fruit. Thank You for not giving up on me! In Jesus' name, Amen.

9

Goliath Had a Brother

Here is the scene: You are in a battle against sickness, oppression or some similar struggle. You seek God, and in some way the grace of God touches your life. Your victory may come through a word or prayer or some other encouragement, but you absolutely know the Lord has delivered you. Using the five smooth stones of divine grace, you have defeated your Goliath.

But then, a few weeks or months or perhaps years later, all the old symptoms suddenly return with a vengeance. If you were struggling with an illness, it manifests itself now worse than ever; if your battle concerned a relationship, it seems as though all progress has been lost and you are back to square one.

Have you ever been there? These negative experiences can drain the faith from your heart. You lose the anticipation and power of faith, and a spiritual paralysis immobilizes your soul. You may still attend church, but your faith is unresponsive. When others testify of deliverance, you worry secretly that they, too, will "lose their healing."

For many, the result is one of faith-shaking disillusionment. Scripture says, "Hope deferred makes the heart sick" (Proverbs 13:12). This "heartsickness" is a spiritual disease that can cripple your walk with God. Remember, faith is the substance of the things you hope for; if you lose hope, your faith becomes hollow. How can you trust God when it seems as though He let you down? You wonder: *Did I lose my breakthrough, or was I only deceiving myself and never really had it?*

Dear one, it is very possible that what you are experiencing is not a loss of God's blessing but an entirely new spiritual battle. This new war is a clever and effective deception that Satan uses to try and worm his way back into the lives of those delivered by God.

I had been praying about this very thing, this recurring battle, when the Holy Spirit spoke to my heart: *Goliath had children.* I was reminded immediately of David's war against the Philistine giant. We all know that David became a great hero by trusting God and defeating Goliath. Later in David's life, however, other giants showed up to war against the Lord's servant. Amazingly, all of them were related to Goliath! Three of these giants were Goliath's actual children; one was Goliath's brother.

> Now when the Philistines were at war again with Israel, David went down and his servants with him; and as they fought against the Philistines, David became weary. Then Ishbi-benob, who was among the descendants of the giant . . . intended to kill David. But Abishai the son of Zeruiah helped him, and struck the Philistine and killed him.
>
> 2 Samuel 21:15–17

After defeating a giant once, David had to face another giant who probably looked just like Goliath. We can imagine that the giant talked like Goliath, fought like him and probably even smelled like him. The text reads, "David became weary." The Bible is silent as to what might have been going through the king's mind that wore him out. Perhaps he wondered, *I thought I killed him. What is he doing back?* Goliath had not come back; he was dead. It was the giant's children who appeared. It just looked like the same battle!

Likewise, you also have had many successful victories. Just because the current giant you are facing looks like the one you defeated in the past, do not buy the lie that you never really won the first battle!

By the strength of God's grace, you trusted the Almighty and conquered your Goliath. The first giant is dead. Satan is masquerading as your former enemy so he can slip past your faith and regain entrance into your life. Resist him. Do not accept the lie that you were never delivered. Stand in faith (see Ephesians 6); our faith is the victory that overcomes the world (see 1 John 5:4). The living God who helped you conquer Goliath will empower you to overcome the son of Goliath as well.

Father, I come to You as Your servant. Like David, I have become weary with fighting an enemy I thought I had defeated. By the power of Your Holy Spirit, however, I expose the lie that this is the same foe I previously conquered. In Jesus' name, I rebuke the enemy. I ask You, Lord, to send angels to strengthen me supernaturally, just as angels often strengthened Jesus. In the name of the Lord, Amen.

10

Overcoming Fear

Have you ever had the feeling that, when the Lord called you to do spiritual warfare, He dialed your number by accident? I know with myself, sometimes I think that if He really wanted someone to fight for Him, He should have saved Attila the Hun instead of me. But then, feelings of inadequacy should be normal, for when it comes to learning warfare, we are all inadequate.

In God's eyes, however, our sense of inadequacy is good. Paul says:

> For consider your calling, brethren, that there were not many wise according to the flesh, not many mighty, not many noble; but God has chosen . . . the weak things of the world . . . and the despised . . . the things that are not, so that He may nullify the things that are.
>
> 1 Corinthians 1:26–28

God cannot "nullify the things that are" with someone who is strong in his or her own strength. When it comes to changing the world, God cannot use strong people who trust in themselves. He chooses weak and even foolish people who know they are inadequate. The weaker we are in ourselves, the stronger He can be revealed in our warfare. He is looking for people who rely upon Him instinctively. People similar to Gideon.

Fear and Oppression: Constant Companions

Just prior to the Lord calling Gideon, a prophet was sent to Israel. Part of the Lord's word through him was "I delivered you . . . from the hands of all your oppressors . . . and I said to you, 'I am the LORD your God; you shall not fear the gods of the Amorites. . . . But you have not obeyed Me'" (Judges 6:9–10).

Whenever we fail to obey the Lord, we begin to fear the power of the gods of this world, and we become oppressed and enslaved by our enemies. Oppression plagues many Christians. In most cases the oppression abides because we have been afraid to face our enemies and deal objectively with our problems. At the same time, the Holy Spirit promises: "You will be far from oppression, for you will not fear" (Isaiah 54:14). But instead of confronting issues in the love and authority of Jesus Christ, we simply adjust our lives to the level of our oppression.

Gideon had made these adjustments to oppression. When the Lord called him, he was hiding in a winepress, beating his grain in secret so the Midianites would not steal it. Gideon, like all of Israel, was afraid and oppressed by his enemies. Not only does fear oppress us, it demands that we labor to fulfill our tasks in the most difficult way possible. For Gideon, it meant threshing wheat in a winepress instead of on a threshing floor. A winepress is an enclosed circular structure; a threshing bin has doors open toward the prevailing wind, which blows away the chaff. It is no easy job threshing wheat in a winepress. When you are fearful, you never live life the way you should.

It is interesting that when the angel sent by God spoke to Gideon, he looked right past Gideon's circumstances and fears, and even past the image Gideon had of himself. He spoke directly to the new courageous person God was in the process of creating. Speaking to Gideon, he said, "The LORD is with you, O valiant warrior" (Judges 6:12).

God saw Gideon as the leader of Israel. In the same way, He sees us as "more than conquerors" (Romans 8:37, KJV). Gideon's response to the "valiant warrior" label is typical of something I have heard often when counseling people: "If the LORD is with us, why then has all this happened to us? And where are all His miracles which our fathers told us about?" (Judges 6:13). Have you ever asked yourself why your Christianity is not working the way it works for others? The Lord's response to Gideon is the same response He gives us: "Go in this your strength and deliver Israel from the hand of Midian. Have I not sent you?" (verse 14).

The Source of Our Strength

Many of us carry oppression in our souls because we have learned to accept the dominance of our spiritual enemy. We want to see miracles and deliverance, but it has not happened the way we expected. Like Gideon, we say, "Why has all this happened to us? Where are the miracles?"

But a new day is occurring. The Lord is training and anointing us for war. Thus, He says to us what He said to Gideon: "Go in this your strength. Have I not sent you?"

Let me explain something vital to accomplishing the Lord's assignment successfully: Our strength is not in ourselves. As

Christians we must draw our strength from our relationship with Jesus Christ. The effectiveness of our authority comes from Him. This is what He means when He sends Gideon, yet says, "Go in this your strength. Have I not sent you?" Those whom the Lord sends, He empowers.

When I was younger, many times I launched out in some project that failed or fell short. Today, I have learned that my strength is in the Lord. I am not anxious to "do something" for God. I give Him time to confirm His assignment to me through two or three witnesses, which may occur over a few days or months. When I travel I go confidently, knowing that this is not my idea, but God's. I travel as the Lord's representative, backed by His strength and anointed with His authority.

To whatever degree I have enjoyed success, I realize it did not come from my personal strength or charisma; I am most successful in allowing myself to be "weak" and trusting God. I honestly do not trust my abilities. I have learned patiently to allow the Holy Spirit to speak and confirm His word to my heart. If He does not give me a new assignment every day, I work to excel in yesterday's task. This resting in the Lord is the basis of all other success.

A friend of mine wrote recently asking for prayer. Everything was falling apart for him, and he felt as though he was holding on only by his fingertips. I told him that it was okay to go ahead and let go, because even if he fell, he would fall into the hands of God. It is that fearful falling transition— that momentary switch from relying on fingernail power to God's strength—that is scary. You see, even if we try and fail, "The steps of a good man are ordered by the LORD: and he delighteth in his way. Though he fall, he shall not be utterly cast down: for the LORD upholdeth him with his hand" (Psalm 37:23–24, KJV).

Gideon had known failure, and bad things had happened. What he had not known was the strength of the Lord, which now approached him. Do not worry about how imperfect you are, which was what Gideon was doing when he complained, "My family is the least . . . and I am the youngest" (Judges 6:15). Our lack of cultural pedigree does not trouble God. He takes us right where we are, and He determines to help us overcome our enemies one at a time.

Gideon, like us, simply wanted God to be God. He repeatedly asked the Lord to confirm His will (see Judges 6:17, 36–40; 7:9–15). As important as it is for us to be in motion, it is just as important to be going the right way. Let God steer you. If in your own strength you run off the road, He will get you back on track. It is preferable, though, to let Him confirm His word so you can know for sure His direction. God likes people who like Him to be God.

The issue is not our ability but our availability. Throughout the whole discourse in Judges, Gideon never said no to God. He proved God, he questioned himself, but he never said no. He continually made himself available to the will of God.

If the Lord calls you to do the impossible, tell Him yes. When you read the Bible and the amazing promises God gives to His children, say yes. Write *yes* at the end of each verse. Align your inner man with God's Word. Even if you know you cannot do it, agree with it. When the Lord tells you He wants to teach you how to do warfare, say yes. He will empower you if your soul is available to Him, but He really cannot use you until you are willing to be used.

The beginning of warfare will awaken your enemies, so expect conflict. The first assignment God gave to Gideon was to pull down the altar of Baal, the Midianite god. When Gideon did so, the townspeople came out in anger to stone him. The name *Baal* means "lord" (one of the devil's names is Baalzebub, "lord of the flies"). There is one true Lord, the Lord Jesus Christ, who sets us free to walk in His victory; there is also a false "lord," the devil, who is the oppressor of both mankind in general and ignorant and fearful Christians in particular.

When you first resist the devil, it is amazing how many of your friends will begin to resist you. When anyone enters into spiritual warfare, good people will ask you to not "make waves" or "make the devil mad." Fear of the devil is a stronghold of oppression in the Church. Do not protect the devil! Gideon's father rescued Gideon and said, "If [Baal] is a god, let him contend for himself" (Judges 6:31). From that time on, Gideon was known as *Jerubbaal*, which means, "Let Baal contend against him" (verse 32). Paraphrased into modern terms, it means "devil fighter."

If we are going to walk in Jesus' victory, we will not only contend against the forces of darkness, but also "tread on serpents" (Luke 10:19). Smith Wigglesworth, the great nineteenth-century evangelist, said, "If God had His way, we would be like torches, purifying the very atmosphere where we go, moving back the forces of wickedness." It is time to stop being fearful and move forward in victory!

Do Not Rely on Numbers

When the Lord finally sent Gideon against his enemies, Gideon had more men than God needed. From 32,000 men, the Lord chose 300. I pray all of God's people realize this truth: The Lord does not need a lot of people to get His job done, just a few who will do things His way. Since my walk with God began, I have never had enough people, money or skill to accomplish what was before me. I have always felt like one of the weak, "base things" (1 Corinthians 1:28, KJV) that God, in His goodness, chose to use. Yet remember the Lord's promise: He chooses the base things and the weak to "nullify the things that are."

Do you see the strongholds of darkness over your city or region? Do not fear them. God says they are going to come down and our land will be turned back to Him. Remember the words of Jesus to His disciples:

> All authority has been given to Me in heaven and on earth. Go therefore and make disciples of all the nations, baptizing them in the name of the Father and the Son and the Holy Spirit, teaching them to observe all that I commanded you; and lo, I am with you always, even to the end of the age.
>
> Matthew 28:18–20

Jesus sent His disciples. His sending them and their subsequent reliance on Him was the basis of their success and the source of their power. He says to us what He said to Gideon, "Go in this your strength and deliver [your people from their enemies]. Have I not sent you?"

Father, forgive me for not accepting Your view of me. You have called me "more than a conqueror." You have said I am a new creation. You have given me Your Holy Spirit and said that all things are possible. I repent of looking to numbers, finances or physical abilities to accomplish the assignment You have given me. I look to You for every victory in my life! In Jesus' name, Amen.

PART 3

Fighting for Our Loved Ones

But as for me and my house, we will serve the LORD.

Joshua 24:15

11

Unwavering Perseverance

If we are to succeed spiritually, among all the other necessary virtues we especially will need perseverance. We will need to learn not only how to fight, but how to keep going in the fight until God brings the breakthrough. I am not talking about becoming carnal in our warfare or fleshly in our aggression. I am speaking about a combination of discernment, authority and unwavering faith that needs to live within us, even while other virtues and gifts develop.

It is not enough, you see, to know about God's Kingdom—we are called to possess it. Yes, when we are born again, we are born into God's Kingdom. But the reality of being born of the Spirit means that a whole new realm of possibilities, challenges and obstacles now unfolds before us. In other words, we must overcome many things in order to function as sons and daughters of God. The idea that the only relationship we have with heaven is the one we experience at death is simply contrary to the Word of God.

When Jesus came, He proclaimed, "The kingdom of heaven is at hand" (Matthew 4:17). *At hand* means that God's Kingdom is close enough to touch from where we are. Yet it must be fought for aggressively and attained with perseverance. "The kingdom of heaven suffers violence," Jesus taught, "and violent men take it by force" (Matthew 11:12).

The violence of taking the Kingdom by force is not physical violence, but rather focused earnestness, a deeply passionate pursuit of God that enables Christ's followers never to give up regardless of the conflicts and trials they face. John said he was a "partaker in the tribulation and kingdom and perseverance which are in Jesus" (Revelation 1:9). If we want God's Kingdom, we will face tribulation, and we will need perseverance. We must persist until the substance of God's Kingdom is not merely a doctrine but a functional reality in our lives.

True disciples "bear fruit with perseverance" (Luke 8:15). The human spirit is saved by faith in Christ's sacrifice. The human soul—our mind, will and emotions—is saved by faith and endurance (see Luke 21:19). This does not mean our salvation is the result of works; it means our perseverance is rooted in our salvation as new creatures in Christ.

Even so, there is a war to be won! We must take the Kingdom by force, fighting for our souls and persevering on behalf of families, cities and nations.

Unyielding Perseverance

The book of Revelation mentions the word *perseverance* seven times for good reason. Over and over we see those who persevered and overcame. It is one thing to have vision and another to have godly motives, but neither will carry us to our objectives by itself. We must also persevere.

Consider this word *persevere*. Its meaning is rooted in the word *severe*. It is the exact opposite of lethargy.

Speaking from experience, I will tell you truly: *There are times when we will not reach our spiritual goals unless we are stretched in ways others call severe or extreme.* En route to victory, our trials may become severe. Likewise, it is with severe faith—severe or extreme steadfastness—that we inherit the promises of God (see Hebrews 10:36). Paul warned that it is "through many tribulations we must enter the kingdom of God" (Acts 14:22). James tells us that "the testing of [our] faith develops perseverance" and that "perseverance must finish its work so that [we] may be mature and complete, not lacking anything" (James 1:3–4, NIV).

In other words, we must be ready to go not just one mile, but two; we contend for the faith; we wrestle against principalities and powers (see Matthew 5:41; Jude 1:3; Ephesians 6:12). We are not wimps; we do not give up. We are soldiers who endure hardship. Even if we are knocked down, defeat is not final; we rise to fight another day (see Micah 7:7–8). Surrender is not an option!

Our success comes from our faith in God; our perseverance is not based on our strength, but is appropriated from grace drawn from our union with Christ. We come to Him when we are weary and heavy-laden; in Him we find rest so we can continue our quest. But underlying all our other virtues, we need to possess an inherent perseverance of spirit. For "the one who endures to the end, he will be saved" (Matthew 24:13).

Has lethargy quietly taken your energy captive? Do you feel defeated by oppression? Then by the grace and supply of God, let the Holy Spirit awaken within you today the perseverance of Christ. Indeed, "may the God who gives perseverance and encouragement" (Romans 15:5) empower

85

you to be the man or woman of God you were born to become.

No Time to Quit

On a more practical level, let me briefly say watch your health. Avoid excessive amounts of heavy foods or white sugar and denatured grains, which can cloud your mind and make you sluggish. Get seven to eight hours of sleep, use natural foods and develop an exercise regimen to tone and condition your physiological makeup. Let's not give ourselves any physical reasons to fail spiritually.

Multitudes will sit in their easy chairs and read about God's promises, but you and I are called not only to know God's promises, but to possess them and walk them out. You see, the real question is not "Are you saved?" but "Are you overcoming?" Whatever the scope of warfare you face—whether it is deeply personal or a fight for your nation to be turned around—the enemy's specific goal is to get you to give up. With all my heart, I believe it is not too late for my country of America and many other nations to turn away from judgment and move toward spiritual awakenings. It is near, dear friend.

Endurance. Perseverance. Steadfastness. These are the qualities that breed character, that transform the doctrine of Christlikeness into a way of life. Again, as James 1:4 urges, "let endurance have its perfect result, so that you may be perfect." The key to perfection, to a life "lacking in nothing," is perseverance.

With the Holy Spirit's help, it is time to get our grit back. It is time to fight.

Lord, forgive me for tolerating a peacetime mentality when I am living in a time of war. Master, I repent of self-pity, of unbelief and of lethargy. With the help of Your Holy Spirit, I drink from the waters of renewal and eternal life that flow to me from Christ, my life. Anoint me again, O Lord, with wisdom and with holy zeal. In Jesus' name, Amen.

12

Your Appointment Awaits You

In spite of escalating turmoil in our world, one last, great outpouring of mercy still remains before the time of the end (see Matthew 24:14; Acts 2:17). This supernatural season is not something for which we must beg God. No, its coming has been predetermined. It is the "appointed time" of the Lord.

For those unaware, an "appointed time" is, in truth, an open display of the sovereignty and power of God. In it we discover with absolute certainty that nothing is impossible for God. It is a season in which He fulfills the hopes and dreams of His people. The psalmist wrote, "But You, O Lord, abide forever, and Your name to all generations. You will arise and have compassion on Zion; for it is time to be gracious to her, for the appointed time has come" (Psalm 102:12–13).

During an "appointed time," it seems as though the Lord rises physically and moves in unfailing compassion on behalf of His people. It is a time when divine promises, dreams and spiritual hopes are fulfilled. Recall that Abraham and Sarah waited in faith for a quarter of a century for the promise of God. Finally, as they neared one hundred years of age, the Lord told them, "At the appointed time I will return to you . . . and Sarah will have a son" (Genesis 18:14). One year later, "at the appointed time" (Genesis 21:2), Isaac was born to his aged parents!

While there are indeed "appointed times" of judgment (see Mark 13:33), the phrase most frequently represents a time, preset by God, when He invades mankind with "wonders, plans formed long ago, [unfolded] with perfect faithfulness" (Isaiah 25:1).

Demons may stand arrayed against the Lord; nations may align themselves to fight Him. It does not matter. He who sits in the heavens laughs, for He makes "all things [His] servants" (Psalm 119:91). Even His enemies' plans for evil are reversed and made to serve the purpose of God (see Genesis 50:20; Acts 2:22–23; Romans 8:28).

If God gave you a vision, a spiritual hope or dream for your future, an appointed time will come when what God spoke will come to pass. Thus the Lord assures us,

> Record the vision
> And inscribe it on tablets,
> That the one who reads it may run.
> For the vision is yet for the *appointed time*;
> It hastens toward the goal and it will not fail.
> Though it tarries, wait for it;
> For it will certainly come, it will not delay.
>
> Habakkuk 2:2–3 (emphasis added)

If you have a vision or promise from God, that vision also has a time of fulfillment. Though it tarries, wait for it. For it will certainly come to pass at the appointed time.

Appointed Servants of God

Prior to the unveiling of an appointed time, God will have been actively working in *hiddenness*. When He rises and moves, He is moving the power grid He has already laid in secret. The work is revealed suddenly, but the preparation may have taken years. Likewise, the Lord also appoints people in whom He has already been at work. He sees the time of their breakthrough in advance, even as He works silently within their hearts in preparation. Consider the Lord's word to His disciples: "You did not choose Me but I chose you, and appointed you that you would go and bear fruit, and that your fruit would remain" (John 15:16).

I am sure the disciples felt that they had chosen Christ. Yet the deeper truth is that God chooses us long before we choose Him. Indeed, "no one can come to [Christ] unless the Father . . . draws him" (John 6:44). In fact, "we are His workmanship, created in Christ Jesus for good works" (Ephesians 2:10). So let's agree with God that He chose us.

Yet He who chose us appointed us as well. Jesus said, "I chose you, and appointed you that you would . . . bear fruit." The same power that worked surrender and inspired faith in us continues to work in our hearts throughout our days, appointing us to bear fruit.

You may look at your life and feel unfruitful. But God is not done with you yet. Do you believe God has chosen you? Then believe, too, that He has appointed you to bear fruit. The same power that drew you to Christ is now working to conform you to Him.

The Enemy's Work

One may argue, "But I know people who were good Christians who have fallen away."

Yes, but in most cases you will find that, at some point, they fell into deep disappointment about some failed spiritual expectation. Disappointment is not just a sad, emotional state of mind; it actually can sever our hearts from faith. It is the enemy's work. Demonically manipulated disappointment can actually "*dis*-appoint" a person from God's destiny for their lives.

I have known many who were doing well, moving toward their appointed destiny. The future God had for them seemed almost close enough to taste. Then they became disappointed in someone or something. By accepting disappointment into their spirits, a bitter cold winter took over their souls, and their faith turned dormant.

When someone is disappointed, he or she is cut off from a scheduled appointment with destiny. The appointment remains in the heart of God, but the individual cannot connect with it because the offense filled his or her soul with unbelief. As a result, the person becomes *dis*-appointed.

I remember a time of disappointment I endured. Indeed, the promise of God was so distant that it seemed like a foolish spiritual fantasy. For nearly three years I had not been involved in pastoral ministry. No doors would open. God was doing a work in my soul, but I did not see it. Then, in what felt like a moment of abject honesty, I prayed, "Lord, You promised that those who believe in You would not be disappointed. Master, You know all things. Look at my heart. I am full of disappointment."

The Lord simply replied, *Your life is not over.*

Of course, I knew that. I was a healthy young man with most of my life ahead of me. Yet the spell of disappointment had flooded my soul with darkness, causing me to conclude erroneously that God was done with me.

The only way Satan can stop our destiny is if we accept the power of disappointment into our lives. Often, it is not blatant rebellion against God that causes backsliding; it is the acceptance of *dis*-appointment into our hearts. Dis-appointment cuts us off from our vision, and without a vision people perish.

Beloved, are you carrying disappointment in your heart? Renounce it. Forgive those who have disappointed you. Pluck out of your spirit the paralyzing sting of disappointment! Today the Spirit of God has come to release you from the effect of this attack. He sent me to tell you, "Your appointment with your destiny is still set."

Holy Spirit, I confess that disappointment has crept into my soul. I forgive those who have disappointed me, and I release them back to You. I also forgive myself for accepting disappointment. I renounce unbelief and submit again to Your call on my life. Lord, prepare me again to move into the future You have appointed for my life. In Jesus' name, Amen.

13

A Word to the Women of God

I want to open this chapter with an important word about women. My goal here is to exalt and release a special grace that God has given specifically to them. It is a powerful gifting that the Lord has used in times past to release revival—and He desires to use it again. Let's start at the beginning.

When the Lord created humankind, He placed unique graces in man and separate but equally unique graces in woman. He told Adam to name the species of life on earth, "and whatever the man called a living creature, that was its name" (Genesis 2:19). This "naming" was much more than calling the dog "Spot." Adam was created with an organizational, administrative capacity that enabled him to identify and define the world around him. By naming the living things, Adam not only brought them into his consciousness, but also introduced order and structure to the human experience. Adam did not create the world, of course, but by defining the things God brought to him, he established reality.

Within the genetics of this original man there also existed the powerful, but dormant, qualities of the woman. While Adam slept, the Spirit took from the man a rib. Fashioning it into a woman, the Lord created for Adam a companion. Not only was she suitable for him, but she powerfully expanded man's creative capacities. Indeed, the woman brought many new graces into Adam's world that did not exist formerly— the foremost of which was the power to conceive and give birth.

This is important to remember: God created male and female in His image, according to His likeness (see Genesis 1:26). In certain ways, of course, both Adam and Eve as individuals possessed reflections of the divine nature. They each could think, speak, dream and create. It was, however, in the *union* of Adam and Eve, in their mutual respect of one another's strengths and graces, that mankind would possess a more perfect expression of the fuller nature of God.

As Adam beheld this first female, he said, "This is now bone of my bones, and flesh of my flesh; she shall be called Woman, because she was taken out of Man" (Genesis 2:23). The term *woman* was a delineation used by Adam, identifying her as a unique variation in the species of man.

My wife says, "Think of her as the upgrade." In some ways, she is right, for the nature of the woman was twice refined. Adam was created of earth; the woman emerged not from the earth but from the man. She is both more complex and more emotionally sophisticated.

Soon Adam began to understand the greatest power of his counterpart—her ability to conceive and bring life into the world. Recognizing this quality, Adam named her *Eve*, which meant "Life." Eve would play an integral part in the unfolding of life's new beginnings. "She was the mother of all the living" (Genesis 3:20).

How Women Affect Revival

The Lord gave Adam a primary ability to name and establish reality; He gave to woman the unique capacity to conceive and then birth reality. The primary strength of each sex is that man establishes, woman births. Remember, these qualities are not merely "human": they are reflections of the divine. Man's ability to bring order to one's world, to take what is random and give it definition and structure, is a divine faculty. Woman's ability to conceive and incubate life, and then deliver life through birth, is also an aspect of the divine nature.

Note also that Adam named the woman *Eve* (or "Life") before they had children. God gave the woman an ability not just to have babies but also to release *life* in a variety of its expressions. In fact, one translation says that *Eve* means "to enliven." Alone, Adam had been downcast; it was not good that Adam was alone. Eve enlivened Adam in ways no other creature on earth could. Adam could build a house; Eve made it a home. When Adam named Eve "Life," not only was he speaking prophetically of the first mother, but he was speaking out of his own experience: Eve brought life into the structure of Adam's world.

We are speaking in generalities here, but when we observe the spiritual realm, we see this same divine encoding replicated in the ministries of men and women. Jesus laid the foundation of the Church with twelve men whom He called to be apostles. This did not mean there would never be women in leadership, but that one of the better skills given man from God was the ability to bring order and structure.

By the same token, prior to Christ's birth we find Anna, a prophetess, engaged in much prayer and fasting. In my opinion, it is quite possible that this woman was not alone in her intercession. I think it likely that she was the leader of a prophetic prayer ministry that lived in anticipation of her times. Women excel in intercession, in spiritual sensitivity and the release of new beginnings. Note: this does not excuse men from prayer! Actually, some of the Bible's best examples of intercessors are men! We are speaking in generalities and making reference to the spiritual tendencies of both sexes. Neither distinction is more important than the other. Both are absolutely vital for the unfolding of God's will upon the earth.

Today we are fighting the advance of Satan in many arenas. Whether the topic is wars and terrorist attacks or the ever-increasing expansion of iniquity in our world, we need revival. To possess a national awakening, the "birthing" power God has placed in women must be released. All the efforts of man to establish laws and govern righteously will not truly transform our culture. We need something greater; we need the presence of God poured out. I believe God is raising up and anointing a prayer army of women who are about to be given even greater power as they intercede before God for their families and their nations.

My Mother's Prayers

I know personally the power of a woman's prayer—my mother's. In the late sixties, I was a very lost young man living in sin and rebellion. Judging from my appearance, I looked hopeless. Yet in spite of my outward condition, my dear Catholic mother stood before God for me. Resist though I did, divine power, uniquely responsive to her prayers, began to hunt me down. Her cries were relentless and unceasing; often she would pray through the night for me. She was pregnant with prayer for her son.

In 1970 God finally answered, and during the Jesus Movement revival I came to Christ. Years later I asked the Lord about this revival. As you may know, it has been part of my assignment to help engender citywide unity and establish prayer, things that precede revival. Yet, to my knowledge, no citywide unity or organized prayer fueled the Jesus Movement. So I asked the Lord how revival could occur without a prayer movement at its source. The Lord quickly corrected me, saying that there was indeed a great prayer movement: He had heard the prayers of a million praying mothers, each crying to Him for her children.

From all denominations, in a "unity of desperation," God heard the cries of believing mothers. His heart was touched, and as a result, multitudes of sinful kids found repentance and salvation in Jesus Christ. This is the army God desires to release again today, but now with more vision, with more power from the Holy Spirit and with the support of men as well!

Women of God, the fact is, heaven needs you! You have been created by the Almighty to birth breakthroughs on planet earth! God has uniquely designed you with a latent ability to release life through your intercession. Together with you, we men can build and establish, and we are learning to pray, but you have a special grace to release new spiritual beginnings. Whether your prayer focus is for your husband or church leadership, whether you are interceding for your children, city or nation, you possess in your spirit the seed-realities that, through prayer, can release God's life into the world.

Yes indeed, a battle rages; there still exists "enmity between [the serpent] and the woman" (Genesis 3:15). Satan especially hates you because it was your seed that bruised the serpent's head. It is amazing to me that God chose to bring His Son into the world, not through the heavens nor even through a woman impregnated by man, but through a woman made pregnant by God! God Himself came to earth through the woman's power to give birth!

Today the Lord is giving women a new grace, a new confidence against the powers of hell. Through their intercession, these godly women will prayer-birth powerful ministries on earth, of both male and female. They will release new beginnings to the Body of Christ.

I also want to commend and personally thank the many women's ministries and prayer groups that have stood with me, interceding for my life, my family and my ministry. Many, many times I have suddenly experienced divine protection or unexpected spiritual breakthrough, and when I questioned the Lord about it, He said, *I'm answering the prayers of [such-and-such] ministry.* To each of you, I say a special thank-you. May the Lord multiply His grace toward you and give you the desires of your hearts!

Revelation 12:1 speaks of a "woman clothed with the sun." This word is not just talking about Israel or the Church. It also reveals how God sees spiritual women: They are honored and crowned with distinction; pure and clothed with the glory of God. With confidence, they tread upon the powers of night. Dear army of praying women, it is your inherent destiny to birth that which shall rule the nations.

Heavenly Father, I come in the name of Jesus. Lord, release the women of God. Release the power of prayer, the burden and travail of prayer, to its next levels. Father, Islamic terrorists from without and moral decadence from within seek to destroy our homeland and families. We need the prayer army to arise. Help us, O God, to pray until Your heavenly purpose is birthed on earth as it is in heaven! In Jesus' name, Amen.

14

Prayer Warriors

In our rapidly changing times, people are desperate to know the future. Barely do we adjust to the last changes when totally new realities explode into our world.

In answer to the common fears spawned by change, society has been inundated by a plethora of occult and demonic sources—fortune-tellers, astrologers, psychic hotlines—all pretending to be able to peek into the mystery of tomorrow. Indeed, how many otherwise intelligent individuals glimpse, at least occasionally, at their "astrological signs" and try to get an edge on knowing the future!

Why anyone would consult someone who cannot predict his or her own future is beyond me. These fortune-tellers almost always live in poverty. Their ability to predict the future should at least work for themselves, should it not? They could invest in the stock market or pick the right lottery numbers. They cannot better their own fortunes, yet people go to them for discernment.

Tremendous Power in a Christian!

Christians must realize that God condemns this demonic, fleshly probing into the unknown. He has called intercessors not to wonder about the future, but to create it through the knowledge of His Living Word and prayer! Our Father gives us access to the future right now. You ask, "How do we know what to pray?" The Lord Jesus has told us plainly, "After this manner therefore pray ye: Our Father which art in heaven, hallowed be thy name. Thy kingdom come. Thy will be done in earth, as it is in heaven" (Matthew 6:9–10, KJV).

We can look at the conditions of the world and faint or look at the possibilities of God and take faith. To bring revival is to pray for the reality of God's Kingdom to be made manifest on earth. Jesus was not offering His disciples a millennial prayer focus, for that rule of God's Kingdom is coming whether people want it to or not! No, Christ calls us to pray for God's Kingdom to manifest itself in our world *today*.

How will tomorrow look if God answers the prayer Christ gave us? Read the gospels. What we see in the life and power of Jesus Christ is a faith picture of God's Kingdom. Jesus said that we can have that same full manifestation. In fact, He actually commanded us to pray for heaven's release!

The Prayer Womb

This Kingdom reality that God has planned will always manifest itself first in the prayer life of His intercessors. When you hear from God and then pray His Word, you are having an impact on the as-yet-unformed essence of life with the Spirit of God Himself! This is why God calls us not only to know His Word, but also to pray it. We must go from intellectualizing God's Word to being impregnated by it.

I know that many churches have special areas where inter-cessors can pray or people can meditate. Maybe we ought to change the name of such places from "prayer room" to "prayer womb." Everything good and holy that we see mani-fested in people, in churches and in life is first conceived and then birthed in the womb of prayer.

We have answers to prayer all around us. The place you are living in is an answer to prayer. When you asked God to lead you to the church you should attend, your current church became God's answer to your prayer. Similarly, your attendance and participation are answers to the prayers of your pastors and intercessors.

Paul wrote,

> I pray that the eyes of your heart may be enlightened, so that you will know what is the hope of His calling, what are the riches of the glory of His inheritance in the saints, and what is the surpassing greatness of His power toward us who believe. These are in accordance with the working of the strength of His might.
>
> Ephesians 1:18–19

If you are a Christian, a power accompanies your life that is greater than great: the "surpassing greatness of His power." It is not human power but the actual "strength of His might." God demonstrated this "power toward us who believe" first "in Christ, when He raised Him from the dead and seated Him at His right hand in the heavenly places" (Ephesians 1:19–20).

In other words, the power of God's might is His resur-rection power. What does *resurrection* mean? It means that things that look dead, smell dead and act dead can be touched by God and raised to life!

Now think about it: The resurrection power God has given us is of the same potency He demonstrated when He raised Jesus out of the grave. Right now, because the strength of God Almighty is attached to our prayer lives, we can look on things that are absolutely dead and pray forth eternal *life*!

Our mission is to bring resurrection life to situations that are dead. If the devil challenges your prayer, remind him that you are seated with Christ "far above all rule and authority and power and dominion, and every name that is named, not only in this age but also in the one to come" (Ephesians 1:21). Christ's authority is final. But not only did the Father put "all things in subjection under His feet," He also "gave Him as head over all things to the church, which is His body, the fullness of Him who fills all in all" (Ephesians 1:22–23).

Notice how the Lord uses anatomical metaphors to explain the downlink of authority: Christ is the "head" of a "body" that has all things put under its "feet." This is a most profound understanding of our role: *What the Head, Christ, has attained, the feet of the Church walk out.* In other words, God has positioned the Church as the living bridge between the terrible conditions on earth and the wonderful solutions from heaven!

As we truly, passionately and accurately submit to Christ in prayer, the Kingdom of heaven steadily enters our now prayed-for world. The key, of course, is to know Christ's Word, for our authority does not originate from ourselves, but from the "sword of the Spirit, which is the word of God" (Ephesians 6:17). What we have is revelation and submission. But as we submit to the Word and persevere in prayer, the future is changed and conformed to God's will.

The devil knows that if he can keep our prayer lives silent, he keeps God's hand distant.

Arise, Prayer Warriors!

When Jesus said we "ought to pray at all times and not lose heart" (Luke 18:1–8), He was saying, in other words, that if we are not praying we will lose heart. Most of the things I pray for I have to pray through to get the answer. God desires to see something deeper come out of my prayer time than just my getting an answer to prayer. He wants me to become like Jesus, so He arranges character-forming battles that will not only change the world around me ultimately, but change me first. This is what all true prayer warriors have discovered.

When we picture a prayer warrior, most of us usually envision a great-aunt or grandmother. I think that every family has one. You never find them looking into a crystal ball to know the future for little Johnny; they are at the throne of God creating Johnny's future in prayer. They are not wondering if Mary is going to make it; they are praying her through to victory. They do not have time to lament Harry's drinking problem; they are storming heaven to see him delivered.

Prayer warriors are the most frightening, powerful, demon-chasing, world-moving beings on earth. In truth, they are co-creators with God! They look at astrological predictions and rebuke them. They never wonder about the future because they are too busy creating it. Prayer warriors are positioned by God to stand in faith for their families and churches and cities. Prayer is stronger than kings and mightier than armies. Prayer is the most powerful force on earth.

I remember when my dad surrendered his life to the Lord. For ten years prior to that, during our annual visits, we clashed intellectually about God. Then one day he came "armed" with an argument many use against God. He said, "If there really is a God, why doesn't He always answer prayer?"

He was secure in his position, and I was tired of the argument. I went into the bathroom and prayed, "Lord, You've got to give me an answer."

When I returned, I could see that Dad felt he had won this round. I love my dad very, very much, so this is what I said: "Dad, forget all the people whom you think didn't get answers to prayer—you yourself are an answer to prayer! You are alive today because our entire family daily prays for you." Then I continued, "But let's experiment. You say God doesn't answer prayer; we say He does. So for one week we won't pray for you, and we'll see what happens."

I cannot remember ever seeing my dad turn so pale. He looked over at Mom and said, "Hon, tell the boy not to do that." Then, with beads of sweat forming on his forehead, he said to me, "Okay. What do I have to do to keep you praying for me?"

In three minutes he went from disbelief in prayer to begging us to keep praying for him. I said, "Dad, the only way I'll keep praying for you is if you pray right now and give your life to Christ." The Lord answered my prayer.

Prayer anchors us in God's strength for our battles. Each of us knows prayer works: We are saved today because someone else prayed for us. As we look at the miracle of our own conversions, we gain confidence in God's help and ability to transform others.

Luke 21:36 tells us to be "praying [in order] that you may have strength to escape all these things that are about to take place, and to stand before the Son of Man." When Jesus says this, He is not talking about the Rapture. Every time the Bible talks about standing before God, it is speaking of a position of anointed authority and commissioning. One who stands before God is an attendant to the Almighty. When that one decrees God's Word, it comes to pass.

Nothing Is Impossible!

God has called you to be a prayer warrior, starting with prayer for those you hold dear. Christ is in you, and He ever lives to make intercession. All you need do is open your heart to Him, and prayer is going to come forth. Look around you at the landscape of life. God wants you to release, through prayer, His future for every need you see. He shows you what is wrong so you can pray for things to be made right. Why waste your energy criticizing people or situations that are wrong, when your prayer can change them!

The Lord our God in the midst of us is powerful. Our weapons are mighty to pull down strongholds. Stop thinking of yourself as unable to pray. That is a lie out of hell. You are a prayer warrior!

There was a time when that great-aunt or grandmother was younger. She was just like you, and God showed her the need around her. His grace came, and she made a decision not to judge but to pray. She did not start off strong, but she became strong. Now it is your turn to make the decision to be a prayer warrior.

Lord Jesus, I choose to follow You. I accept that You have called me to be a prayer warrior. By Your grace, I receive a new anointing in intercession to pray especially for those I love. In Your name, Amen!

15

Fighting for Our Families

In this chapter, I want to broaden the voice of the family and ask my wife and one of our five children to join me in this discussion about fighting for our families. First, I will write from a husband and father's viewpoint; next, Denise will share a wife and mother's perspective; then our oldest, Joy, will communicate her heart to those praying for their children. The impetus for much parental prayer in her younger years, Joy is now the mother of two children herself and understands the power and importance of a parent's prayer from both sides of the family circle.

Francis: Growing as Head of the Household

Being a good man in the twenty-first century is hard enough; being a godly husband and father is a real achievement. As men, we are supposed to be tough, but we also have to remain tender and sensitive. We have to know how to administer our authority, yet we must do so with encouragement and love.

We cannot be without convictions, but we also must walk in compassion. Which all goes to say that, like most men, I have made a lot of mistakes.

One thing I have learned is that no amount of premarital counseling can prepare a couple for marriage or provide all the answers for raising a family. The complexities of the human personality expand beyond our ability to prepare for the roles of husband and father. We will all make many mistakes while living with the personalities, needs and desires of other people. So when I talk about fighting for our marriages and families, I am speaking specifically about overcoming the areas of our own immaturity that would otherwise erode our ability to love. This means we must stay humble in our opinions and learn to listen to others when they tell us how we may have failed.

I grew up the oldest of three sons. My mom was a sweet Italian lady whose parents were born in Italy. She was the tenth of fourteen children and was raised with the understanding that the man was head of the household. Dad was the breadwinner; Mom was the homemaker. What Dad said was law, and Mom seemed perfectly content with it. It was the way life was.

I did not date in high school and had only one semi-serious, mostly disastrous relationship prior to meeting my wife-to-be, Denise. My problem was that my expectations of a woman's role as wife were all shaped by my mom, who was submissive, loving and quiet, and a great cook. In the Francis Frangipane dictionary, next to the definition of *woman* was a picture of my mom.

I met Denise in 1971 and immediately led her to the Lord. A few months later, we were married. Denise was a Jersey gal. Did I mention that she was also a hippie who thought that being rebellious was a virtue? I tried to help her understand

God's Word, especially Ephesians 5:22, where Paul teaches, "Wives, be subject to your own husbands." Denise did not get it. Not only that, but she could not cook.

What she and I both had, though, was a reverence for God's Word. Scripture said that what He had joined together, no man could put asunder (see Matthew 19:6, KJV). We could not solve our differences with divorce—and we loved our children. We also knew God loved us, and once we determined not to quit, we discovered that the Lord was always there to help us.

The key is to walk humbly. We all make mistakes, and when we do, we need to admit them and ask for forgiveness. I do not believe most people intentionally hurt each other, but hurts do happen. A careless word or the extended neglect of a relationship can create pain. To heal relationships, we have to heal the pain we caused. Once we win the trust of our loved ones, we can cultivate the love that is actually still there.

Today our marital relationship is priceless. I love my wife more today than at any time in our marriage. We both have had to find the place of humility and forgive one another. But there is a reward from God that comes just for enduring. It is the reward of the two becoming one. It is the stuff heaven is made of.

Our five children are grown now. When they were growing up, however, at least twice a year I had a private meeting with each one of them in which I asked where I had failed them. Their usual response was to evade giving an answer. Instead, they would affirm that I was the best dad, blah, blah, blah! Since I knew I was not perfect, I had to probe them a little, until they actually opened up and spoke candidly. Inevitably, it turned out I had said something that embarrassed them in front of their friends, or perhaps I had failed to adjust my father-child relationship with them appropriately as they grew older. After they told me what I had done wrong, we prayed together. I asked for forgiveness and we went on from there, reconnected in love and life.

Again, humbling ourselves—yes, even to our kids—and asking for forgiveness does two things: It helps us stay united, and it establishes love again where perhaps there was pain. The apostle John said, "I have no greater joy than to hear that my children walk in truth" (3 John 4, KJV). Amen.

To help us understand the battle for our families in more depth, I turn now to my wife, Denise, and to our daughter Joy, who will give her testimony concerning the Lord's grace in our lives. Joy has become one of the closest people to me in my life, but it was a fight for us to find each other's hearts. Their stories will encourage you not to give up in the battle for your own family.

Denise: Loving "Self" Less

How does a good relationship survive when, by nature, we are basically selfish, self-centered creatures? Born in sin, we are bent toward evil. Our flesh nature is greedy, covetous, dominating, physically abusive and proud—and those are just a few of our flaws! We have to die to self so that Christ, in His perfect nature, can live in us and flow through us to each other and to our children.

For me, marriage was not only the beginning of my walk with God—having met the Lord the same time I met my husband—it was also the beginning of death to self. Having five children quickened the process.

Not only did marriage and having children mean giving up sleep and sharing my bed, bathroom and food, it meant giving up the right to myself. What I wanted was no longer a priority; I had to consider my husband's wants and my children's needs.

Family life is demanding. From the physical weariness of taking care of little ones to the mental drain of dealing with the teen years, it can be a fight just to hold on to your sanity. It is hard to say how many tears we shed over the wrong things we did and the regrets we had. In many situations, we wished we had done things differently. But all any of us can do is try our best and trust God, who causes all things to work for good (see Romans 8:28). God is good. Every right thing that we did impart to our children will hopefully come to fruition in their futures.

But family life is rewarding, too. It is worth it all. Every bit. My relationship today with Francis and my children is the closest thing I have to heaven. I love them all so much it hurts. I still tend to worry about them, especially the kids, but I know that God is in control. The most important thing I can do for them is pray with all my heart, with faith, and believe God will do the rest. (Okay, we still send the children money, too.)

For our marriage, God's grace is there when we need it. We have both changed so much in the last forty years that I can only thank the Lord. Of course, forgiving each other helps release us to keep growing. Along with the humility Francis mentioned, forgiveness is also key to building and maintaining a healthy relationship. God gives us the grace to survive the many difficulties we face. Both of us are passionate Italians. When we were first married, the minister looked at us and said, "Nitro, meet glycerin." Yes, there were some explosions along the way, yet we have stayed committed through it all. We are blessed to be together and to see the fruit of God's grace: Our love is stronger than ever.

Through the years, Francis and I have watched many couples break up, couples who were seemingly much more compatible than the two of us. Yet they gave up. They failed not because they did not love each other, but because they were not determined to fight and endure until they reached the blessings God had in store for them. It is that holy fight that kept us reaching for the best things God could give us.

Joy: Watch the Seeds Grow

No one can tell me that fathers and daughters cannot have close relationships or even become best friends. People are almost envious of the love my dad and I share. The only thing we argue about is who loves whom the most.

Our relationship was not always this warm. There was a time when I felt I had lost my ability to love my father. I was a teenage Christian in a public high school. My Christian background made me different. I was new, and at a time when I most craved acceptance, my father's rules seemed to be the source of my rejections.

Fueled as I was by my insecurities, in my eyes my dad became the root of my problems. While I felt I set an adequate standard and struggled to live by it, he was strict. I was angry because he refused to back down from the standard he knew was right. He refused to compromise with my ignorance in order to gain my acceptance.

Things were going from bad to worse during those years. We hit bottom the day I looked him squarely in the eyes and told him that I hated him. Those were harsh words, but it was a hard time. I did not really hate him. I hated *me*. I felt I was not bad enough to be accepted by my friends and was not good enough to be accepted at home. When these feelings take over your life, you search for something—anything—to blame. I chose my father. He carried the brunt of my pain. He even became my enemy.

In my heart I knew I did not hate my dad. I was angry and confused. I thought that he was not concerned with how I felt. It seemed he had made no room for compromise with my situation. Yet he was willing to risk losing my love to save my soul.

It was a hard time for us both. He suffered the pain of rejection, as I did. He suffered the hurt and the loss, but from a different angle. His fear of the Lord helped him withstand his fear of pain. He loved me, but he had a higher obligation to meet than my favor and my approval. I am sure at times he wondered if he was doing the right thing.

There must have been times when my father felt as if his prayers were hitting the ceiling and bouncing back at his feet. At times I am sure he considered lowering his standards to meet mine. It would have made things so much easier than wrestling with the power of an independent, strong-willed child. These considerations may have come to his mind, but he never gave in to them. He stood firm and prayed harder.

The prayer of a righteous man avails much (see James 5:16). Many times Dad cried out to the Lord in anguish and in frustration, "What have I done wrong?" Today my father has a wonderful ministry to God in prayer. I think I had something to do with the character God worked in him during those days. Before he ever prayed for cities and nations, he was on his face praying for me.

"Train up a child in the way he should go, and when he is old he will not depart from it" (Proverbs 22:6, NKJV). That verse was a promise that my dad held on to. "Your sons and your daughters shall prophesy" (Acts 2:17) was another promise he stood on. He had given me to the Lord and had set a godly standard, so he held God to His Word.

At the same time, I was wrestling with my salvation. My desire to be accepted by my non-Christian friends at school warred against my desire to be with the Lord. James speaks of a double-minded person being unstable in all his ways (see James 1:8). I was completely unstable. I walked on a line between heaven and hell. I wanted the best of both worlds and was satisfied with neither.

Although I had been brought up in the Church, the world had taken its toll on me. My eyes had been blinded to the sin in my own life, further separating me from God and my parents. It was so hard for me to see my way out.

When a child is brought up in a Christian home, regardless of what may happen, the seed that has been planted in his or her heart continues to grow. It is an amazing seed because it can grow in the dark without water; it can even bloom in adversity. The reason we can never outrun God is because He is that seed growing within us. Once you have tasted the presence of the Lord, nothing satisfies you as He can. You can run to other things, but you know they are not what you long for. Sometimes those who seem to be running the hardest from God are doing so because He is so close to them.

On the outside my witness was weak, and I was in bondage to my unsaved friends. But on the inside, my heart cried for oneness with the Lord. I hated my double-mindedness as much as my father did. My whole life, I wanted strong Christian friends to save the world with me. I wanted the support, I just never had it. I did the best I could with what I had, but I lost my sensitivity to sin. The more I was with non-Christian people, the more deceived I became.

Paul warns, "Do not be deceived: 'Bad company corrupts good morals'" (1 Corinthians 15:33). I did not realize the impact my unsaved friends were having on me. The more I was with them, the more I conformed to them. When I look back, I know that if my parents had not been praying for me, I would have been on my way to hell.

Sin has a way of moving in and taking control. But love is as strong as death; many waters cannot quench love. And love never fails. (See Song of Solomon 8:6–7; 1 Corinthians 13:8.) Prayer is the highest power through which love is released, and my parents prayed faithfully for me. Yet I had to relearn how to love. My love had become completely self-centered and conditional. I had failed to realize that my father and my Lord loved me unconditionally. I had only to try. I had only to bridge the communication gap to understand that God had loved me before I was even aware of His standards. And my dad loved me for me alone, not for something I had to become.

My relationship with my father is wonderful now, and that is the truth. God has proven Himself faithful working in both our lives. The Lord has bridged the gap between us and filled it with love. It took leaving my non-believing friends and being planted with Christian people who faithfully loved me. It also took my willingness to change, but it did happen.

Please do not give up on your teenagers. Do not sacrifice God's standards of righteousness to appeal to their carnal nature. They cannot respect you for it, and God will not honor it. Your children were not consecrated to Satan; they were dedicated to the Lord. He has had His hand on them, and He will not forget them. He has heard your prayers and is faithful to your cries. He is God.

Prayer works. I am living proof of it. I look back now and see how many times nothing but the miraculous dedication of loving parents took me out of hopeless situations. The Lord will not forsake His children. He will not turn His back on them. We are never too far from His reach. Believe the promises of the Lord. He is not a liar. He honors a steadfast heart. Hold on. Your children will come back to the Lord.

Master, the enemy has attacked our homes and led many of our children away captive. God, restore our families to Your design. Grant grace to see our homes reflect Your heavenly life and potential. Master, forgive us where we have fallen short with each other. Grant new beginnings to Your people, especially among spouses and parents and children. May it be true of me and my household that "we will serve the Lord." In Jesus' name, Amen.

PART 4

Fighting for the World around Us

There is none like the God of
Jeshurun,
    Who rides the heavens to your
help,
    And through the skies in His
majesty.
The eternal God is a dwelling place,
    And underneath are the everlast-
ing arms;
    And He drove out the enemy
· from before you,
    And said, "Destroy!"

Deuteronomy 33:26–27

16

The Real Jesus

Not only is Jesus our Savior, He is also the "author and perfecter of our faith" (Hebrews 12:2, NIV). Grab with both hands the thought that He is the "perfecter of our faith." The faith Christ started in you, He is now working to perfect.

The fact that Jesus is the "perfecter of our faith" is important because even if we seek to move in prayer and spiritual authority, even if we fearlessly continue to persevere, even if we continue forward with motives purified by love, it is the power of faith that undergirds all.

Now the idea that Christ seeks to perfect our faith makes a fine doctrine, but in the practical outworking of our lives, we deeply resist the idea. For we know that faith, in order to be perfected, must be tested.

When I speak of faith, I do not mean a thorough compilation of Bible facts or an intellectual assent to our need of salvation, both of which are elements of spirituality, but not the very substance. To amass biblical knowledge primarily takes time; to possess true saving faith, I will tell you again, takes courage. Christ desires we obtain a trust in Him that can actually withstand and overcome the terrible storms of life—faith that brings the reality of heaven to earth.

Faith, therefore, is more than head knowledge; it is our lock upon the goodness and power of God so that no matter what we face outwardly, inwardly we stand secure. And no matter what the world looks like outwardly, it has the potential to be transformed by our faith. As Hebrews 11 makes clear, all those who possessed true faith changed the world around them.

Perfect or Protect?

Knowing that faith is much more than religious doctrines, I wonder, do we truly know the Jesus of the Bible and what He seeks to give us? Too often, I think, we desire a Savior who, after assuring us of eternal life, leaves us alone until our next crisis. We want Him to comfort us but never convict us; we desire Him to heal us but not inhabit us. In my country, for example, we tend to want the Holy Spirit to help us obtain the "American dream." Yet what we have is a Holy Spirit who, instead, seeks to give us the dream of God: *man living in the image of Christ* (see Genesis 1:26).

This means that God's goal is not merely to save us, but to conform us to Christ. He seeks to perfect us, not merely protect us. To perfect faith, God intentionally allows conflicts to storm against our souls.

I know we picture Jesus as gently holding us, patting us on the back, saying, "There, there, it'll be all right." Listen, that is not the voice of Jesus; that is the echo of your mother speaking. Thank God for mothers, but Jesus is seeking to get us to stop being such babies. He wants us to grow up into His image.

120

Remember, I am talking about the real Jesus now, the one who said, "All things are possible to him who believes" (Mark 9:23). If the Jesus you are following is not leading you into the realm of the impossible to make changes in your world, you are probably following the wrong one.

You see, we do a disservice to people when we tell them, "Give your life to the Lord, and He will keep you from trouble." That is not true. We would be more honest to say, "Give your life to Christ, and He will empower you to overcome trouble and adversity." Yes, He will take care of you. But He will not do so by putting you in a harmless world void of problems. Rather, He will perfect virtue in you by developing character and by requiring faith—all of which creates the spiritual shelter of a transformed life.

A Storm, a Ghost or Jesus?

Get used to the idea that Jesus is seeking to perfect your faith. Plan on the fact that He will probably set you in some otherwise impossible situation to force your faith to the surface. Sooner or later, the real Jesus will require you to look the impossible straight in the eye and believe God for His power.

Consider the incident when Christ sends His disciples on ahead of Him by boat across the Sea of Galilee and chooses to cross the sea Himself on foot (see Matthew 14:22–33). He decides to wait until a storm is rolling in with contrary winds and waves before He sets out. He could have waited for a calm day or simply arrived at the other side supernaturally without stopping alongside the boat in the middle of the sea. No, He comes to the disciples with something in mind: He comes to teach a lesson on trust.

Please note that this is a violent storm and that He offers no preliminary instruction, no "Basic Water-Walking 101."

121

He does not let them practice on puddles or wait until winter so they could walk on frozen water first. He waits for a storm to teach water-walking, which is by all accounts harder to do on rolling waves than on a placid sea. Then, on top of that, He does not come in daylight; He comes at night. So Jesus comes to the disciples in the middle of the sea, in the middle of a storm, in the middle of the night to teach them to walk on water. He does not make it easy. But this is the real Jesus with His real disciples. And we can add to the degree of difficulty the probability that they are physically tired and more than a little fearful about the storm.

Scripture says that the sight of a figure walking on the water, coming out of the blowing wind and spray in the darkness of the night, turns the disciples' fear into terror. They cry out, "It is a ghost!" (Note: Some of the things we label as "ghostly" or demonic are really the Lord stirring life to set the stage for a lesson on faith.)

As Jesus approaches the rolling boat, He calls out, "Take courage, it is I; do not be afraid."

When Jesus says in the midst of your storm, "It is I," it is a call to faith. When He says, "Take courage," it is a call to action. True faith will always, at some point, require courage.

Peter says, "Lord, if it is You, command me to come to You on the water."

This is wonderful, really. Here is an insight not only into Jesus Christ, but also into Peter's relationship with Jesus. Ever since Peter has known the Lord, Christ has required him and the disciples to do impossible things: heal the sick, feed multitudes with a lunch pail of food, raise the dead. Over and over Peter has seen Jesus work miracles; over and over Jesus has empowered Peter to do what he saw Jesus just do.

That night on the stormy sea, Peter shows this amazing discernment: "If it's really the Lord, He will tell me to do what He is doing—something impossible. If it's the Jesus I know, in a moment He will be telling me to walk on the water, too."

And true to form, Jesus calls out to Peter: "Come!"

Now Peter is not about to walk on the water, not really. When he steps out, he is walking on the word *Come*. He knows that the power to accomplish the impossible resides in Christ's word, and it is this supernatural reality upon which he steps.

You see, this is all about trusting the integrity of Jesus Christ's command. Do you think Peter feels power when he steps on the water? I do not think he feels anything besides the storm. No goose bumps. No "glory chills." Peter sits on the topside rail of the rocking boat and swings his legs over the churning water. Peering through the wind and rain, he looks at Jesus. Then he slips down, stands upright in the water and begins to walk!

Splash! One step. Splash! Then another and another until Peter walks right up to Jesus. This is no little walk. Admittedly, anyone can walk on water for the first step. It is the second step and beyond that is difficult. Peter walks until the waves grab his attention; then he begins to sink. Jesus saves him, of course, and when they get into the boat the wind stops.

Maybe we would expect the Lord to say, "Peter, you did it!" Maybe Peter was expecting praise for his short water-walking career, but no, Jesus rebukes him, asking, "Why did you doubt?"

Christ sees the beginning of something great within Peter, and He does not want it contaminated by pride or self-pity. Most of us want a medal every time we do something for God, but He is not about to let Peter or us build a monument to our accomplishments, especially when we are just beginning. If this miracle of Peter's were done by some of us here in America, in two weeks we would have tours, T-shirts and commemorative celebrations of the day we walked on water. But Jesus will allow none of that for His disciples. He sees greatness emerging in Peter, and He will not press any of His disciples toward anything other than full conformity to His image.

Remember: God's goal is that we become Christlike. The real Jesus is going to call us to do the impossible. This means that we will be called to do what we have never done before.

You will see Jesus ahead of you, probably in some kind of storm, but it will be the beginning of a miracle that will change you—and the world around you.

> *Lord, forgive me for seeking a safe life instead of a supernatural life. I want more of You. Call me out of the boat of my familiar, predictable world. Master, for the sake of reaching the lost, increase my faith until I am standing with You on the water of divine potential. In Jesus' name, Amen.*

17

Will Jesus Find Faith in You?

Do you see the importance of faith in our fight for all that we hold dear? We desire to see the world we live in transformed. God wants to move us forward into a future full of glorious possibilities, not fears.

Some argue that fear is an ally in bringing men to repentance. Yes, fear is a policeman that keeps us from sin, but it cannot lead us to Christlikeness. Fear moves the soul, but it is only temporary; it cannot sustain righteousness or create true purity of heart. I totally believe and delight in the fear of God, but even holy fear must be the companion of a heart that sees the treasure before us and sells all to possess it. Otherwise we will remain ever trembling.

"Amazing grace" may teach our hearts to fear, but remember, that same grace relieves our fears. The fact is, people are already afraid. It is time for faith to arise, for us to put our trust in God's goodness and power. Miracles are waiting to happen.

Jesus said "all things are possible to him who believes" (Mark 9:23). I think we need to approach the near future, say the next fifty years or so, with transforming faith that confirms all things are possible. I have heard an argument against this approach. It says: "At the end of the age, world conditions are going to collapse. To believe for transformation is to fight against God."

Listen, as long as the true Church is still on the earth, there will never be a time when transformation of nations is impossible.

"What if we are raptured?"

Then the Church will not be here and revival will not occur. But as long as we are here, there is hope for the world around us, and anyone who tells you otherwise is lying.

"Wait, Jesus said there would be wars. How can there be revival and war?"

Yes, Christ warned: "When you hear of wars and disturbances, do not be terrified; for these things must take place first, but the end does not follow immediately" (Luke 21:9). He said specifically, "Do not be terrified." Do not submit to the spirit of terror—have no part in it! "God has not given us a spirit of fear, but of power and of love and of a sound mind" (2 Timothy 1:7, NKJV).

Now if you are not terrified or fearful, what are you? You are believing God for something great.

In Luke 18:8 Jesus asks a question: "When the Son of Man comes, will He find faith on the earth?" I am amazed at how people almost deliberately misinterpret this verse and then use it as a justification for their unbelief! They say, "See, it says right here that we will not have faith."

No, it does not. As we have noted about this portion of Scripture, Jesus has just given a parable to show His disciples that at all times they ought to pray and not to lose heart. He then encourages His disciples, saying that God will speedily avenge His elect who cry to Him day and night. His question is just a question, not a statement of fact. He is asking if He will find faith. The answer we give is not theological but personal: It is based on whether we have faith or not.

If you answer Christ's question about faith with an unbending "No, the elect won't have faith at the end of the age," beware. This doctrinal deception justifying your unbelief will eliminate you from becoming one of God's elect. You see, the elect have faith. They cry to God day and night, and He answers them "speedily."

Prayer and Faith

I am a man of prayer. It frightens me to think of a life without prayer, for prayer is, at its core, communion with God. Yet there is a difference between prayer and faith. We need both. I know people who pray but do not believe. They discern no evidence in their spirits that God has heard them or that He will answer their prayers, yet they pray. Because they have no faith, they are without confidence. They talk to God, but to them He is more like a bartender than the Lord of Hosts. They pour out their problems to Him and feel better temporarily, but no faith in them has been activated; they do not expect anything to change.

So we need prayer, but we also need faith. How can we get faith? "Faith comes from hearing, and hearing by the word of Christ" (Romans 10:17). Faith does not come by cerebrally reading the Bible, but by actually hearing, in the core of our hearts, what Christ is promising us as His followers. He said all things are possible to him who believes, and He said faith in God is so powerful that it can move mountains (see Mark 9:23; 11:23).

127

My faith tells me that God desires to reach all the nations of the world and break the strongholds of darkness that blind cultures to the Gospel of Christ. I believe that this is the highest passion of His heart and that everything going on in this world, from heaven's view, is working to fulfill this worldwide outreach to the lost (see Matthew 24:14).

Even when mistakes have been made, God is causing all things to work for the good of His purpose to reach the lost. Ultimately, that makes the war against Islamic terrorism not merely about oil or expanding democracy or ending radicalism, but somehow about nations becoming more receptive to the Gospel of Jesus Christ. It means that the globalization of nations is not just about commerce, but about removing barriers so people can hear the Gospel. It means that the Internet and satellite television were invented not just to expedite world trade, but to enhance outreach by Christians.

One could certainly argue that the forms of media in our world are evil. Many are tangled in the web spun on the Internet by dark minds; the proliferation of pornography is a tragic example. And there is no doubt that greed is rampant throughout the world system. Yes, hell has a way of seizing and exploiting opportunities, almost making it appear that the discovery of technological realities was Satan's idea. It was God, however, who created the world that science is discovering; and it was God who authorized that, at the end of the age, "knowledge will increase" (Daniel 12:4).

What I am saying is that God's heart is reaching to the nations. We need to be aware of and engaged in this awesome display of divine compassion. Every day, we should be praying that laborers be sent forth from nations around the world, for indeed, the harvest is plentiful.

Cleansing Starts at "Home"

Speaking in reference to my homeland, America, I believe the Spirit of God desires to turn this nation toward Him. A great many of America's political leaders are Christians who have accepted a call from God and believe passionately in a holy destiny for our land.

America has sinned against the Lord, granted, but so had Israel under King Saul. And when the Philistines sent Goliath to terrorize Israel, the Lord did not say, "Too bad, but I have sent this giant to defeat you because you are sinners." No. The Lord raised up a deliverer, a young man named David, who loved the Lord and knew God's heart. David challenged his adversary, "Who is this uncircumcised Philistine, that he should taunt the armies of the living God?" (1 Samuel 17:26).

Perhaps most of Israel was sinful at that time. Obviously all were fearful about confronting Goliath. Yet one young soldier was righteous. God's eyes were not on the fearful, but on the fearless. The Lord was not planning on destroying His people, but raising up a leader who would lead them in faith and triumph. Do you see this? God used the righteous to deliver the unrighteous. He can do the same in our nations today.

The Lord allows enemies to smite a nation when there are no deliverers, no righteous souls willing to resist the evil in their land. If there are righteous people, He makes them deliverers and warriors. He increases their strength and influence. He assures us that where sin abounds, grace abounds all the more!

Today God is giving grace to those who love Him. It is not time to fear; it is time to stand before the Lord prepared, spiritually clean and ready to fight in faith.

Lord, I want every thought, every breath to be an expression of my faith in You. Lord, deliver me from a passive, unbelieving heart. I position myself at the throne of Your abilities. Hear my cry when it rises. I want to be a believer, not a "make-believer." In Jesus' name, Amen.

18

When David Captured Jerusalem

One of the errors of the Church is to limit the expectation of our faith to what God did with previous generations. It is not wrong to want what others had, but God actually has more for us than what occurred in past eras. Indeed, many promises concerning the Church are yet to be fulfilled before Jesus returns. The Bible tells us that the Church will experience not only "perilous times" in the last days (see 2 Timothy 3:1, KJV), but seasons of renewal and restoration (see Acts 3:21). Consequently, in the midst of worldwide conflicts, the Kingdom of God on earth will continually be restored and renewed until it is conformed to the Kingdom of God in heaven! Plan on seeing new harvests and expressions of God's glory and power. We should expect to see wonders that our fathers did not see (see Acts 2:19–21)! Yes, and let's also trust that the promises we fail to possess, our children will walk in.

We can find encouragement and guidance once again in the life of King David. He was born into a time similar to ours. The Hebrews were in the Promised Land, but they shared the land with unconquered enemies. When David became king, he knew that God had promised more for Israel than the Jews had attained. In particular was the fact that the Jebusites still occupied the area now known as Jerusalem. Now, if David had measured himself by the success of his predecessors, he never would have contemplated an attack against the Jebusites. The Jebusites were a fierce mountain people, and in spite of being on the list of nations to be dispossessed by Israel, they had never been conquered.

Think of it: Israel's greatest heroes from Joshua to the judges had tried and failed to conquer the Jebusites. Thus, the Jebusites were contemptuous when they heard of David's plan to possess their chief city, Jebus (Jerusalem). They mocked Israel's young king, saying, "You shall not come in here, but the blind and lame will turn you away" (2 Samuel 5:6).

There are two lessons here. First, for everyone who desires to see the awesome promises of God fulfilled, God is saying to us all, *Don't be conditioned by the past!* Just because you have not seen the manifest power of God over your church or city or nation, do not take that as a forerunner of things to come. God can change everything overnight.

The second lesson is this: It probably will not be the devil himself who comes out to defeat us; rather, we must guard against the misguided advice of unbelieving Christians. Remember, the taunt of the Jebusites was that the "blind and lame shall turn you away." We may stand firm in faith against the spiritual hosts of wickedness, only to be defeated by the spiritually "blind and lame" sitting next to us in church.

Who are the blind? Put simply, they are the ones who do not see the vision you see. They are blind to the faith-future God has put in your heart. We cannot let people who do not see our visions become our counselors. Beware of becoming sympathetic toward the spiritually blind. A little leaven of their unbelief can undermine your faith in a time of battle.

Along with the spiritually blind are the emotionally lame. These are people who have stumbled over something (or someone) in the past. They no longer walk stride for stride with Christ. Beware of sharing your dreams with cynics. If we heed the warnings of the "lame," it will only be a matter of time before their woundedness and lack of grace depletes our strength. Then we, too, will become overly cautious and suspicious.

Although we need counsel from other Christians, and we must remain forgiving and kind toward those in opposition, we cannot allow the words of the spiritually blind and the emotionally lame to guide us.

These individuals are not our enemies. In our world, our real enemies are the spiritual forces of evil influencing our communities. And let's remember that if we are suffering from being lame or blind, Jesus can heal us. But the fact is, like those Jebusites, Satan has watched the failures of many Christians before us. One can sense the devil's scorn as pastors and intercessors pray for citywide or national revival. The devil's taunts are not without substance, for generally speaking, our spiritual forebears did not succeed in dislodging the strongholds of wickedness from their cities. History is indeed on the adversary's side.

But God has given us His unalterable, immutable Word. He promises:

> For the vision is yet for the appointed time;
>> It hastens toward the goal and it will not fail.
>> Though it tarries, wait for it;
>> For it will certainly come, it will not delay.
> Behold, as for the proud one,
>> His soul is not right within him;
>> But the righteous will live by his faith.
>
> Habakkuk 2:3–4

To "live by faith" is to believe God until the vision He gave comes to pass. David believed God, and in spite of history being on the side of the Jebusites, we read: "Nevertheless, David captured the stronghold of Zion" (2 Samuel 5:7).

There was something in David from his early years that urged him toward the goal of victory over the Jebusites. In fact, Scripture tells us that when David was still just a youth, after he killed Goliath, he took the "Philistine's head and brought it to Jerusalem" (1 Samuel 17:54). At that time, Jerusalem was called Jebus and was occupied by the Jebusites. It was as though David were saying, "Okay, I'm just a young buck, but I've conquered this Philistine giant. Remember me, I will be back." Fewer than twenty years later David returned, now as king of Israel. As he had conquered Goliath, so he conquered the stronghold of the Jebusites. It was renamed the "City of David," though it soon became known as Jerusalem.

This is not about the fulfillment of our lives, but the fulfillment of God's Word. God's Word cannot return to Him void without fulfilling the purpose for which He spoke it. When King David heard the taunts of the Jebusites, he did not draw back in unbelief; neither was his faith crushed because of his ancestors' failures. Instead—and this is important—David interpreted the battle in light of the promises of God. At stake was the integrity of the Lord's personal promise to Abraham and to his seed: "Your descendants will take possession of the cities of their enemies" (Genesis 22:17, NIV). While the enemy may have had history on its side, David had the unalterable Word of God on his side!

It is the heritage of Abraham's spiritual offspring to bring the prevailing influence of God into their communities and, through Christ, possess cities. That is not my word or yours, but the promise of God Almighty! He said it and He will fulfill

134

it. His people shall possess the gates of their enemies. It is a reproach to us that the devil wants our cities more than the Church does! David's desire for Jerusalem was a godly desire that came to him from Christ, for what outwardly was to become David's city was soon to become the city of God.

As David simply believed God's promises, so also must we. The Lord has sworn that "nations will come to [our] light" (Isaiah 60:3). Whom shall we believe? The report of the Lord or the words of those who refuse to see the light? Shall we take counsel from the blind if they cannot see the potential we see? Let's take God at His word. Let me state this again: Jesus Himself assures us that "all things are possible to him who believes" (Mark 9:23). Do you believe? Or are you just a nice unbeliever who goes to church?

Beloved, if we fail, it is no great shame. We simply join the ranks of the spiritual heroes who went before us and "died in faith, without receiving the promises" (Hebrews 11:13). In truth, it is better to die in faith than to live in doubt. But consider: What if we succeed? What if, through the process of believing God, He imparts to us Christ's perseverance and His character? What if we find God helping us to see our cities healed and our nations turned?

Lord, You have promised that nations shall come to our light. Forgive me for wavering in unbelief and for allowing yesterday's failures or attainments to precondition me! I believe that You have prepared our nation for great things. We will follow Your promise to dislodge our enemies, even as David conquered the great city that would bear the name Jerusalem! In Jesus' name, Amen.

19

Hastened in Its Time

The Bible references many subgroups of people, each identified with distinct characteristics. Among them all is one group that heaven refers to as overcomers. They are not perfect, but when they stumble, they get back up. When they have drifted off track, they return to the narrow way. They are shaking off slumber, dissipation and weariness. Though some battles take longer than they anticipated, they are steadily defeating sin and the devil. They have fought to keep their love alive and their vision fresh. They are increasingly becoming wiser and more enduring.

Jesus first referred to this group as His "little flock." Though embattled, they still follow Him wherever He goes. The Father has "chosen gladly" to give them His Kingdom (Luke 12:32). It is my honor to encourage these people, these disciples in search of Christlikeness. I firmly believe that you, in fact, are one of these overcomers. From among those like you will come a new generation of leaders. They will serve God in the next great outpouring of the Holy Spirit. You have been created and destined to influence the world around you.

Many of you are already aware of this calling. For those of you who feel that you lack the means to make a difference in the world, let me tell you again that we are all called to be overcomers. The time to grow is now. Do not worry if you feel that you have lost time. God has allowed for an acceleration in the growth rate of our spiritual lives.

Accelerated Righteousness!

I do not know one church leader who does not believe we are living in the end times. Exactly where we are along heaven's prophetic timeline is debatable; everyone has his or her own catalog of signs that confirm the end times. If we have, let's say, a generation or two left to us before the end of the age, we should expect to see a divine hastening of spiritual realities.

I like to quote Isaiah 60:1–3 often since it points to a great manifestation of the Lord's glory in the end-time Church. Isaiah's revelation concludes in verse 22 with this added encouragement: "I, the LORD, will hasten it in its time." Let's personalize this promise. *The Lord is saying that our transformation will be accelerated in the days ahead!*

Consider also Paul's word: "For the Lord will execute His word on the earth, thoroughly and quickly" (Romans 9:28). There is no reason the Lord cannot do things more quickly should He choose to—He created the universe in six days! I love the idea that the end times are not just about God moving quickly, but also about His accomplishing a deep and thorough work in us. Indeed, if we want the quick, we must focus on the thorough. Yet His promise is for both a quick and thorough work!

> Who has heard such a thing? Who has seen such
>   things?
> Can a land be born in one day?
> Can a nation be brought forth all at once?
> As soon as Zion travailed, she also brought forth
>   her sons.
>
> Isaiah 66:8

I know that, in spite of such promises, many are wearied with battles and delays. Yet the Lord says a time is approaching when there shall no longer be any delays: "As soon as Zion travailed, she also brought forth her sons." Prayer warriors, this is why we must prevail in prayer!

The New Testament uses two words to describe the concept of time. *Chronos* refers to chronological time, while *kairos* is usually translated "fullness of time." Kairos times are those unique, spiritually heightened bursts of spiritual fulfillment that exist between dispensations and epochs.

During kairos seasons, the Spirit of God invades the fabric of life itself. Everything accelerates and changes as reality is redirected to serve the unalterable will of God. Noah lived in a kairos time. Moses led Israel out of Egypt during a kairos time. Jesus came in "the fullness of the time" (Galatians 4:4). So significant was His life that today even the non-believing world marks its calendars from His birth. Such is the impact of kairos upon the affairs of man!

It also amazes me that Jesus was able to take common, nonreligious men and, in just three and a half years, transform them into powerful representatives of His Kingdom. These apostles healed the sick, raised the dead, had deep spiritual substance and wrote Scripture under God's inspiration. How did common men mature so fast? The answer is that the Lord hastened their growth "in its time." They were alive during a period of kairos.

Imparted Life

The apostles' rapid growth did not occur because they were born with superior intellects, enabling them to grasp and quickly implement Jesus' teachings. They were alive during a kairos time, yet their greatest strength, obviously, was their direct relationship with Jesus. The Lord not only trained them by word and example, He also imparted His anointing to them through the Holy Spirit. The result was that the disciples were doing the same miracles that Jesus did. By Pentecost, these common men were mature spiritual leaders, graced with spiritual authority and meekness, committed to prayer, unity and the demonstration of the Spirit with power.

Everything we have in Christ comes to us by impartation through the Holy Spirit. Jesus said of the Holy Spirit, "He will take of Mine and will disclose it to you" (John 16:14). This disclosure of Christ's life through the Holy Spirit is the basis of our relationship with Jesus. The Spirit gives life as we read the Word, and it imparts life in our quest for Christ's likeness. Our relationship with the Lord is not merely theological or cerebral, but functional and substantial.

Jesus was speaking of the effect of this impartation when He assured His disciples, "The works that I do, [you] will do also" (John 14:12). Through the Holy Spirit, the effect of Christ's impartation would continue even after Christ's death and resurrection. Amazingly, though Jesus Himself would be seated in heaven at the Father's right hand, impartation to His disciples would continue "even to the end of the age" (Matthew 28:20).

The proof that we have truly received Christ's anointing is that we have power, at least in some measurable way, to do what Jesus did. The anointing on us is the extension of the anointing on Him. Christ's goal is to replicate His ministry through us via the systematic and revelatory teaching of His Word and by His example portrayed in the gospels, all of which is made alive by the indwelling work of the Holy Spirit.

At Pentecost we generally focus upon the disciples speaking in tongues, but what emerged was much more profound. Through the Holy Spirit, Jesus imparted apostolic leadership to His disciples, steeling them with His own unbending character. The Spirit of God actually became the invisible leader of the Church. Spiritual signs and wonders followed to confirm the disciples' authority.

When the Spirit is poured out during a kairos time, those from within the Church community will work miracles. My point in this is that we, too, are alive during a kairos time. More prophecies have been fulfilled in our days than at any time since the first century. But just being alive during such a time is no guarantee that we will have power like Christ's. The gateway to power—to accelerated growth—is to become serious and committed to being true followers of Jesus Christ. If we want the anointing that worked through Jesus, we must heed the teaching that came through Jesus as well, for His words "are spirit and are life" (John 6:63).

As you and I rivet our lives upon conformity to Christ, His power may manifest through us in serving others. Or it may emerge in our prayer life or our study of God's Word; it may unfold in compassion for the sick or concern for the poor and needy. The anointing may come in a variety of other ways, but it is the anointing of Christ on our lives that defines and empowers our sense of purpose on earth. Whether we serve as a teacher, pastor or evangelist, whether our call is as a student, housewife or marketplace minister, "of His fullness we have all received, and grace upon grace" (John 1:16).

140

Old Testament Roots

The reality of impartation was not a new concept introduced in the New Testament. We also see vivid examples of the transference of anointing in the Old Testament. Whenever we see impartation at work, we see the rapid advancement of spiritual growth. Consider that Elijah was one of the most intense prophets in the Old Testament; his protégé, Elisha, was a farmer. The two could not have been more different. Step for step, the sons of the prophets watched Elisha follow the great prophet Elijah. Elisha's goal was not just the appropriation of information from Elijah; he sought a "double portion of [the] spirit" that rested upon the man of God (2 Kings 2:9). He was in earnest pursuit of Elijah's anointing.

The anointing on Elijah's life was symbolized by his mantle. This mantle is what Elijah used to cover his face when the Lord drew near on Mount Horeb. When Elijah first approached Elisha, he actually "threw his mantle on [Elisha]" (1 Kings 19:19). In so doing, he invited Elisha to receive the best he had. He was saying, in effect, "If you can keep up with me, you will not only become my successor, but I will give you my anointing." From that moment, Elisha became his constant companion.

As Elijah's ministry on earth was drawing to a close, he approached the Jordan with Elisha at his side. In the distance, the sons of the prophets watched in earnest. Taking his mantle, Elijah struck the river, and he and his protégé crossed on dry ground. As they were going along and talking, the Lord suddenly called Elijah home in a whirlwind. As he was lifted by the wind, his mantle fell from his shoulders. Elisha took up the mantle and walked back to the bank of the Jordan. He struck the waters, just as Elijah had done, and said, "Where is the LORD, the God of Elijah?" (2 Kings 2:14). Immediately the Jordan parted, and he walked across the dry riverbed.

The text continues, "Now when the sons of the prophets who were at Jericho opposite him saw him, they said, 'The spirit of Elijah rests on Elisha'" (verse 15).

The sons of the prophets could tell that Elijah's anointing (or "spirit") rested upon Elisha because Elisha did what Elijah did. So also with us: Through our union with Christ in the Holy Spirit, people should be able to discern that the Spirit of Jesus rests on us. In fact, even when we see the Lord's anointing on another believer, we should not consider it inappropriate to ask for training from that believer.

Of course, we need to be cautious. Jesus warned that false prophets would arise in the last days and mislead many. As a safeguard, we should look, first of all, for the character and nature of Christ in an individual before we seek impartation from that person. Do not be intimidated or afraid to ask hard questions of such an individual. Look for tangible fruit. Avoid anyone who is overly focused on attaining wealth or who displays an extremely authoritarian approach to life. We do not just want power; we are seeking Christlikeness. Hebrews tells us to consider the outcome of a leader's way of life and "imitate their faith" (Hebrews 13:7). We are not to imitate such a person's mannerisms or weaknesses, but rather imitate the quality that drew the functional anointing of Jesus Christ into that leader's life through the Holy Spirit. If our focus is right, and if we are not naive, through impartation we can see the acceleration of growth in ministries during this kairos time.

The House of the Lord

Among all the awesome realities that will emerge at the end of the age, we will also see the restoration of the house of the Lord, both in purity and in unity. The foundation of Christ is being restored. As a result, we will again see the fullness of Christ's anointing in the Church (see Isaiah 2:2; Acts 3:21; Ephesians 4:11–16).

I know that the anointing the Holy Spirit put on me to rebuild the house of the Lord is a living power. Now and in my remaining years, communicating this vision to others is and will continue to be the passion of my life. Through our online training school, through utilizing the Internet and television, as well as through conferences and the printed word, I seek to inspire as many people as I can.

What will any of us achieve by returning to Christ-centered, citywide unity in our churches? God's Word tells us that as His house is restored, then "the Lord, whom you seek, will suddenly come to His temple" (Malachi 3:1). The hastening work of God will occur through the Church.

Is this not exactly what we so desperately desire—that the living God will be revealed through us? That when we lay hands on the sick, all of them will recover? I believe a time is coming when ambulances will stop at churches before they go to emergency rooms! God is waiting to accompany our efforts to reach our inner cities. He seeks to raise up and send powerful teams of missionaries into the Muslim world, just as He sent His early disciples into the lands of the unredeemed. They will go forth healing the sick, raising the dead and proclaiming that the Kingdom and goodness of God are at hand.

As the house is rebuilt, the living God will begin to accompany our efforts. Look at His words through the prophet:

> Then I will draw near to you for judgment; and I will be a swift witness against the sorcerers and against the adulterers and against those who swear falsely, and against those who oppress the wage earner in his wages, the widow and

the orphan, and those who turn aside the alien and do not fear Me.

Malachi 3:5

Let's purge our focus off the multitude of distractions and lay hold of that anointing to build God's house. The Holy Spirit repeatedly tells me, *Do not focus on the fearful things around you, the threats of terrorism or economic collapse. Focus steadfastly upon your transformation!* Again, He says, "For I, the Lord, will hasten it in its time."

> *Lord, come quickly. Move speedily in the transformation of my soul. Master, I see the lost around me, and I desire to touch them with Your power and grace. Like Paul, I desire a demonstration of Your Spirit and power, that people's faith would not rest on mere knowledge but on the power of God. Do Your great work quickly and thoroughly in my life. In Jesus' name, Amen.*

20

And Then the End Shall Come

It is no secret that we live in prophetic times. Besides two world wars, earthquakes, famines and floods, our generation has seen the return of Israel to its land and the spectacular increase of knowledge and travel (see Daniel 12:4). While in this great season of spiritual acceleration, we must stay balanced and in sync with the heart of God concerning the world around us.

When Jesus spoke of the signs of the end, He warned that false movements would arise. He said, "See to it that you are not misled; for many will come in My name, saying . . . 'The time is near.' Do not go after them" (Luke 21:8). Since the earliest days of Christianity, people have been caught up in false anticipation that the time was at hand. Even today, while we are certainly much further along than those early believers, we simply have not yet entered the time of the absolute end.

Consider the MESSAGE translation of Luke 21:8–9:

> Watch out for the doomsday deceivers. Many leaders are going to show up with forged identities claiming, "I'm the

One," or, "The end is near." Don't fall for any of that. When you hear of wars and uprisings, keep your head and don't panic. This is routine history and no sign of the end.

Jesus also said that certain events would occur that mark the end times, noting that "these things must take place first" (Luke 21:9). If mankind's journey over the last two thousand years were mapped, prophetic signs are like towns we pass through, helping us to approximate where we are as we approach the Lord's return. They also keep us from assuming we are further along than we are.

There are two major end-time road marks that we have not yet passed through: The Gospel of the Kingdom has not been proclaimed "to all the nations" (Matthew 24:14), nor has the Antichrist been revealed (see 2 Thessalonians 2:1–3). Both of these things must occur before Christ returns.

These Two Major Signs

The worldwide proclamation of the Gospel, which is perhaps the most important sign of the end, has yet to be accomplished. Jesus said that after the Gospel of the Kingdom of heaven is proclaimed "in the whole world as a testimony to all the nations, . . . then the end will come" (Matthew 24:14). In other words, the Good News of God's love for man will precede the bad news of the Lord's judgment upon sin and evil.

Ahead of us will be the world's greatest season of harvest. We will see many hundreds of millions come to Christ from India, China and throughout Asia. The Muslim world will also experience a great multitude of conversions. Africa, which has been last and poorest among the continents, will be ablaze with the outpouring of the Holy Spirit. Black African missionaries will be among the greatest leaders the Church has ever known. I believe even Europe will experience

And Then the End Shall Come

a resurgence of true Christianity, which will bring millions into the saving knowledge of Jesus Christ.

Today reaching and gathering this great harvest is the most fervent passion in the heart of God. Everything that is occurring in the earth today must be interpreted in light of God's heart to bring redemption to the unsaved world.

Nor has the other major sign preceding the Lord's return occurred: the emergence of the Antichrist. While the spirit of the Antichrist has empowered "many antichrists" since the first century (1 John 2:18; 4:3), the Scriptures explain that a singular leader will arise. The world can change rapidly, and we must stay alert regarding the positioning of this individual on the world stage.

Listen to Paul's warning in his letter to the Thessalonian church concerning the "coming of our Lord Jesus Christ" and the timing of the Rapture (2 Thessalonians 2:1). Speaking as a father to a church he loves, Paul expresses a deep concern that they "not be quickly shaken from [their] composure or be disturbed . . . to the effect that the day of the Lord has come" (2 Thessalonians 2:2). The Thessalonian Christians were anxious, for a report had gone forth saying the Rapture had already occurred and they had missed it. Paul is seeking to break the power of this deception.

> Let no one in any way deceive you, for [the day of the Lord] will not come unless the apostasy comes first, and the man of lawlessness is revealed, the son of destruction, who opposes and exalts himself above every so-called god or object of worship, so that he takes his seat in the temple of God, displaying himself as being God.
>
> 2 Thessalonians 2:3–4

When Paul speaks of "the day of the Lord" (verse 2), he is referring to the timing of the Rapture, which the Bible refers

147

to as the "gathering together" of the saints to Christ (verse 1). He says plainly that the day of the Lord will not come unless the Antichrist is revealed.

So before the Lord returns, we can expect the worldwide proclamation of the Gospel to get increasingly more pure and more powerful. In resistance to this great last days' outpouring, Satan will raise up and empower the Antichrist. And somewhere in the sequence of these two events, God will not only restore Israel to its ancient borders but restore Israel to Himself.

Has the Antichrist Arrived?

Much speculation has gone on about the appearance of the Antichrist. Is he really moving among us today? Over the last forty years, Christians have identified many people as the Antichrist—from John Kennedy, to the last three Popes, to Kissinger, Gorbachev and even recently Prince Charles, plus a dozen others in between.

In our anticipation—or fear—how often have we issued false warnings at the expense of our credibility? While many false prophets operate under the influence of the Antichrist spirit, presently no singular religious or political leader can command the actual worship of most of the world. Remember also that the Antichrist will have seemingly godlike powers. He will have been healed from a mortal wound to the head. And he will have a worldwide following. These signs are plainly revealed in Revelation 13. Certainly, preparations seem under way for such a personage to arise and world conditions cry for such a person, but the Antichrist has not been revealed, not according to the signs provided in Scripture.

Consider also the unmistakable characteristics Paul lists in his description of the Antichrist. This man, who will embody

Satan himself, "opposes and exalts himself above every so-called god or object of worship." To demonstrate his so-called divinity, he actually sits in the "temple of God, displaying himself as being God" (2 Thessalonians 2:3–4). The Antichrist will sit in the Holy of Holies in the heart of the Temple of God. This may happen sooner than we imagine, but let's realize with clarity of mind that the Al-Aksa Mosque is currently secured on the Temple Mount in Jerusalem. Beloved, *there is not yet a Temple in which the Antichrist can sit*. So until we see the Temple restored, we should not be preoccupied with speculations about the Antichrist.

Let's also not forget that part of the Antichrist manifestation will be a restriction on commerce. The Bible says that to purchase goods during his reign, everyone will be forced to possess a number, which will be tattooed on either a person's forehead or wrist (or embedded in a chip?). This technology is certainly developing, but we can still buy things with cash. I do not think a mandatory switch to a cashless society will occur any time soon.

Some Christians have written that the euro (the common currency used in most of Europe) is the currency of the Antichrist. God's Word says "all" nations will be economically connected commercially by the Antichrist, not just Europe. The fact is, China, North and South America, Russia, India, Africa and the Islamic world have no plans for the euro. There is no worldwide currency, no mark of the beast. Due to the current financial instabilities, a movement is underfoot that could perhaps culminate in some standardization of currencies. Let's keep our eyes watching for such an event, but it has not happened yet.

In fact, the person described as the Antichrist in the Bible has not emerged. No current leader has been mortally wounded by a blow to his head. There is no Temple in which the Antichrist can sit as god. So regardless of who informs you of his or her secret insight that so-and-so is the Antichrist—whether it is the *National Enquirer* or your favorite Christian author—remember, the Antichrist, when he appears, will be unmistakable and obvious to every true Christian. Whether you ascribe to a pre-, mid- or post-tribulation Rapture of the Church, the Antichrist must come first.

The Real Problem with Predictions

I am in my fourth decade of service to Christ. During this time, I have often seen Christians excited about end-time prophecies that have little to do with the end times. When Christians accept and then broadcast prophecies based upon someone's dream or fear or math, and when these aberrant prophecies fail to come to pass, it is like spraying the unsaved with repellant. They think we have a form of insanity that plagues us with anxiety disorders. They will have none of it.

The problem is that in the 1970s and '80s, many Christians (including yours truly) believed the Lord was coming most any day. As a result, we turned our backs on our governments and school systems. We abandoned our responsibility to be salt and light in the world. Amazingly, after we left the world system, we then condemned the world for its lack of godliness. Here in America, we were so eager for the Lord's return that we could forecast nothing but the judgment awaiting this country! As a result of believing a lie, we suffered spiritual paralysis. This allowed laws to be changed and our nation to slide into great perversion and moral anarchy—all because so many of us thought we were at the end of the age. What a travesty!

If the Rapture of the Church occurs tomorrow, wonderful! We need, however, to pray, plan and act as though we expect to see several worldwide awakenings—waves of redemption—

before Christ returns. I know that a number of us believe in the "seventh day" theory, the idea that there have been six thousand years since Adam and that a seventh "day" is at hand (the Millennium day of Christ's thousand-year reign). I am slaying some sacred cows here, but according to the Hebrew calendar, we have at least a couple hundred years before we reach the year 6000.

I am not saying all of this so we relax, but so we can fully embrace God's call that we become Christlike. You see, if we accept the idea that nothing remains for us but the apostasy and then the Rapture, we exempt ourselves from fasting and praying for our communities. If we have passed the season for revival, then why lay our lives down for cities and nations, especially if God has no intention of redeeming them?

Beloved, until the Lord comes, we need to think and act like laborers in the great end-time harvest. If we focus upon becoming Christlike and seeing the lost come to God, we will not be deceived; we will be fully prepared when the Lord returns. God is reaching for my country and yours. He wants to see godly leaders raised up, inner cities filled with the outpouring of His love and grace and our families healed and restored.

If we truly desire to accelerate Christ's return, then we must complete our part of the prophetic plan, which is to win the lost. It is time for laborers to be trained and sent. Every nation must hear the Gospel, and each soul written in the Lamb's Book must be saved—"and then the end shall come."

Lord, forgive me for looking beyond the immediacy of Your assignment for me. Help me to support with prayer, finances and effort the glorious task of reaching the nations of the world. Lord, also upgrade my life to the standards of Your Kingdom. Deliver me from the cultural boundaries of visionless Christianity. Lead me to Your version of the Gospel, which requires my all but gives me Your best. In Jesus' name, Amen.

21

Prophet, Priest and King

We see that we are not yet crossing the finish line that marks the end of life as we know it; we are nonetheless in a season of spiritual acceleration. Yet regardless of where we are in the sequence of end-time events, our goal is always to reveal the character and power of the Lord Jesus Christ. But what does it mean to unveil the nature of the Messiah?

We use many descriptive terms to refer to Jesus (*Yeshua* in Hebrew)—Lord, Redeemer, King, Savior to name just a few. Most often with His name, we use the term *Christ*. This comes from the Greek translation of the Hebrew word for *Messiah*, which means "the Anointed One." Thus, it is perfectly accurate to call Him "Jesus the Anointed One."

Where does the phrase *Anointed One* come from, and how is it particularly relevant to our witness to the world?

In Bible times anyone could anoint and refresh his or her head with oil. Yet only a special blend of spices and oils was used as "holy anointing oil," and then only in sacred ceremonies (see Exodus 30:22–31). It was copiously poured upon the consecrated individual, perhaps a quart or more, until it flowed down his head, beard and even to the hem of his garments (see Psalm 133). It was an obvious outpouring of oil, not merely a dab on the forehead as is our custom today. Additionally, anointing with oil was done with solemn prayer and reverence, for it was through this ritual of anointing that Israel's prophets, priests and kings were identified and then dedicated to God.

The act of anointing a chosen leader with oil was a ritual pregnant with the hope of Messianic fulfillment. Anointing a prophet, priest or king was a foreshadowing of the ultimate prophet, priest and king to be unveiled in the ministry of the Messiah. His anointing would not be with oil, but with the reality the oil symbolized: the "Holy Spirit and . . . power" (Acts 10:38; see also Luke 4). For all the diversity we see in Jesus' ministry, everything He accomplished was rooted in the soil of His prophetic, priestly and kingly roles.

It is vital for us to understand the nature of the anointing on God's Son because through it we peer into the anointing of God for His Church. All that the Messiah was as prophet, priest and king is still active and is still being transferred to His Church through the Holy Spirit. The Word says, "For of His fullness we have all received, and grace upon grace" (John 1:16).

Our relationship with the Messiah unfolds in two ways. The first is His position over us as our prophet, priest and king. The second is His position as Lord and Master who seeks to train us and impart His very anointing to us through the Holy Spirit. Thus, God desires that His Church—the Body of the Anointed One—be manifest in the earth in three distinct, yet interconnected, ministries that are a continuation of the Messiah's nature as prophet, priest and king.

Messiah as Priest and Prophet

The priestly ministry of the Lord is one of intercession and redemptive sacrifice. The Messiah, as our great High Priest (see Hebrews 3:1), rendered Himself as our "guilt offering" (Isaiah 53:10). He is the "Lamb standing, as if slain" before the throne of God (Revelation 5:6). Because we are created in His image, we also partake of His priestly role of intercession. We become His living house, which is "a house of prayer" (Isaiah 56:7). He calls us to be a "kingdom [of] priests" and a "royal priesthood" (Revelation 1:6; 1 Peter 2:9).

As priests, we receive the offering of the Lamb Himself as a sacrifice, both for our sins and also for the world around us. The Messiah is our great High Priest living in heaven; the Church reveals in her priestly role on earth the intercessions of the Messiah. It is the same anointing, poured upon the head and flowing down the body. The ministry of the high priest has been fulfilled by Jesus, the Messiah. It is embraced and followed by all who are being conformed to Him on earth.

Jesus was also God's prophet. His prophetic anointing enabled Him to x-ray the thin veneer of human respectability; He perceived the secret realities of men's hearts. He understood their unseen sins and fears, shame and dreams. At the same time, He saw into and understood the deep mysteries of God's heart. The Messiah understood God's Word, not merely in its skeletal form of doctrines, but as the union of the Father's living consciousness with His own thought-life. The things Jesus heard the Father say, He Himself said. He was the prophet spoken of throughout the Old Testament by Moses and others (see Acts 3:22), and He was much more— He was the Word of God made flesh (see John 1:14).

As such, His prophetic nature enabled Him to stand beyond the boundaries of time. He could pierce the enigma of ages past and also herald the wonders of times still to come.

Just as His priestly role of intercessor has been extended to His Church, so His prophetic ministry is imparted to us. It is written of Him that He gave "some as prophets" who, though imperfect, also burn with the flaming sword of God's Word (Ephesians 4:11; see also Luke 11:49; 1 Corinthians 14; Revelation 11).

In this regard, He sends out His commissioned ones with the assignment to "make disciples of all the nations . . . teaching them to observe all that I commanded you" (Matthew 28:19–20). When we go forth on His behalf, "whoever speaks, is to do so as one who is speaking the utterances of God" (1 Peter 4:11). The prophetic word that we hear and communicate is, in its purest unveiling, an extension of the living and written Word, which originates from Him.

Messiah as King

The Church is learning, in varying degrees, how to take part in Christ's priestly and prophetic ministries. Our participation in His "kingly" or governmental authority, however, is another story. Many Christians do not believe that the Body is supposed to serve in any leadership positions outside of the Church. They question the legitimacy of Christians serving in secular positions of influence, particularly in the political arena. The idea of our being granted rule and authority has been either deferred to the Millennium or scorned as heretical "Kingdom now" theology, which teaches that Christians must conquer the world before Jesus can return.

Our quest is not to see the Church become political, but to see the political become spiritual, where the integrity, wisdom and justice of Christ Himself manifest in secular leadership. This is not about our ambitions, but about our yielding to the Messiah's anointing for godly rule.

156

For those of us who say Christ's kingly anointing is reserved only for the millennial age to come, let me remind you that Christ is King right now, and our call is to grow up "in all aspects" into Him who is our head (Ephesians 4:15). Right now, Jesus is seated as King on God's throne; He has received "all authority . . . in heaven and on earth" (Matthew 28:18). And we are told specifically: "As He is, so also are we in this world" (1 John 4:17; see also Ephesians 1:18–23; Revelation 17:14). We are to be conformed to His image in all things (see Romans 8:29).

These are "present tense" promises, not only millennial. We must, therefore, measure the stature of the Church by the dimensions of Christ: Is Jesus prophet, priest and king right now in heaven? Absolutely! Then it is God's will that He should be revealed as prophet, priest and king on earth through the Church. This is the very thing we are asking each time we pray, "Thy Kingdom come. Thy will be done, on earth as it is in heaven"!

All that Christ is in heaven will, in varying measures, be manifested in the true Church before Jesus returns. Will there be a greater fulfillment in the age to come? Of course. But just as He has emerged in the Church as priest and prophet, so must there also be some fulfillment of His governmental authority in this present age.

What our Father desires to reveal through the Church is not about us; it is about the manifest destiny of Jesus, His Son. Just as some of us are called to reveal Christ the intercessor and others are sent by God to manifest the life of Christ the prophet, so also shall the unveiling of Christ's governmental authority come forth in chosen leaders at the end of the age.

Many Christians who resist this transference of Christ's governmental authority to the Church, where Christians serve

God in societal leadership, ask for New Testament teaching to confirm this doctrine. "Why didn't Jesus tell us to run for office?" they ask.

In the time of Christ, the world was ruled by kings and those appointed by kings with jurisdictional authority. You could not "run" for the office of king. To do so was called "insurrection." The means to access these places of authority, which clearly was God's will, was to pray for "kings and all who are in authority" (1 Timothy 2:1–2). In a democracy, however, we can field godly individuals to serve the greater community. To be conformed to Christ calls us to reveal His nature as a ruler. Thus, we must accept that it is the destiny for some in the Church to reveal Christ's character in governmental leadership.

Some argue that when politics and religion mix, they become toxic. On the contrary: "When the righteous increase, the people rejoice, but when a wicked man rules, people groan" (Proverbs 29:2). When the righteous rule, justice is served, the poor are defended and the defenseless are protected.

Yes, Christians in government have made mistakes. We should learn from past mistakes but not abandon our destiny because others have failed. My nation was founded by godly men. Many of the signers of America's Declaration of Independence were not only Christians but ministers of the Gospel! (See www.wallbuilders.com.) Many of the first Christians who came to America knelt on its shores and covenanted with God for this land. I pray that in our generation, Americans would not be staggered by unbelief, but rather would pray with faith, "Be [it] done to me according to your word" (Luke 1:38).

Another argument goes like this: "The realm of secular governmental authority is fraught with the corrupting influence of power. Why would God send His servants into secular leadership?" God specifically sends His servants into world systems to transform those systems and lead nations toward heaven.

Consider the eleventh chapter of the book of Hebrews. From verse 22 through verse 34, each person named as an example of faith was an individual raised up by God to lead a nation. Who would like to inform the righteous kings of Judah, from David to Josiah, that it was not God's will for them to be in power? Whisper this idea that God does not anoint and send people into world leadership to Daniel and see if he concurs. The Lord God has always had it in His heart to raise up men and women who serve Him in wisdom and righteousness. These, in turn, He uses to bring multitudes to Himself.

To be conformed to Jesus is to walk in His anointing (see 1 John 2:6). As we near the end of the age, the true Church will be increasingly identified by Christ's threefold anointing: We will be given to intercession as a priesthood of believers; we will be prophetic in our discernment and communication of God's Word (whether the Word comes to teach, comfort, evangelize or warn); and in all of life's spheres, we will walk in a holy, kingly anointing as ambassadors of Christ and His kingship in heaven (see 2 Corinthians 5:20). More on the wisdom of this in the next chapter.

For our world to recognize true Christianity, it must witness one reality: people becoming Christlike in prayer, in the prophetic word and in governmental authority (see Ephesians 4:15). Where the true Church is growing in maturity, it will be united in the full anointing of Christ. And transformation will follow.

Lord, I pray for all who are in public offices, especially those who call upon Your name. Help me to see the union of the prophetic, priestly and kingly anointing as key to transforming our nations. Rule, O Lord, in the midst of Your enemies. In Jesus' name, Amen.

22

A Generation of Rulers

Today, God is raising up warring priests who intercede for mercy; He is anointing prophets and preachers who call His people to repentance and vision; and He is preparing leaders who will rule righteously with wisdom and meekness. The Lord's goal is to manifest the fullness of Christ in the Church, and in so doing, to transform our society.

The final key to our success is the release of godly leadership. Consider God's promise to Abraham:

> As for Me, behold, My covenant is with you,
>> And you will be the father of a multitude of
>> nations.
> No longer shall your name be called Abram,
>> But your name shall be Abraham;
>> For I have made you the father of a multitude of
>> nations.

I will make you exceedingly fruitful, and I will make nations of you, and kings will come forth from you.

Genesis 17:4–6

For more than two thousand years, from Abraham to Christ, God worked primarily with Israel and its line of kings. His promise to Abraham, however, was that he would be the father of "a multitude of nations." He then added, "and kings will come forth from you" (verse 6).

Please listen prayerfully to this promise, that kings will come forth from God's chosen. It has always been in God's heart to bring nations to Himself, but it was not until Christ came that the grace of God could truly spread worldwide. The fact is, you cannot bring nations to God without turning the government of those nations to God as well. So the Lord tells Abraham, "Kings will come from you." Kings exercise authority over nations. Paul speaks of this, in principle, when he urges "that entreaties and prayers, petitions and thanks-givings, be made on behalf of all men, for kings and all who are in authority" (1 Timothy 2:1–2).

In the Lord's promise to Abraham, the Hebrew word for *kings* refers to "officials of many levels." This word *kings* (*melek* in Hebrew) was the usual term for any mag-istrate (*Zodhiates Hebrew-Greek Keyword Study Bible*). In other words, among those who were to come forth from Abraham would be a generation of godly leaders whose sphere of influence would be felt in every strata of secular authority!

Isaiah 60 also speaks of "nations" that would come to our light and "kings" to the brightness of our rising (verses 1–3). Again, *kings* is the same word that encompasses all levels of secular authority.

This promise of God is vital for today, a time when "dark-ness will cover the earth and deep darkness the peoples" (verse 2). Just because the cultural atmosphere is charged with demonic darkness, it does not mean the Almighty has abandoned society.

161

Our Goal: National Transformation

People argue that "if God is going to bring revival, He will do it through the Church." Of course He will, but who says that the Church cannot raise up leaders who will serve with integrity in secular leadership positions? If Christians are in government and we live in a nation where the priestly and prophetic role of the Church is maturing, there remains potential for the leadership role of Christ to be manifested also.

Imagine the heavenly potential when, instead of dividing because of differences, the Church honors the intercessory, prophetic and kingly nature of Christ, as Jesus is manifested in His Body! Imagine when these three streams of anointing converge and, in unity, serve God to bring justice, mercy and healing to their cultures!

Remember, we are not talking about typical church revival. It is good to have times when we break out of our passivity or oppression and find release in God. But we are seeking a nation transformed. We need godly people to serve in elected office. How important is the role of the kingly anointing? *There never was a revival in the Old Testament that did not manifest through the authority of the secular leader, the king!*

When we discuss fighting for those we love and for the lost in our world, we are not talking about praying until we are exhausted or hoarse. We must also have long-term plans, especially in democracies where officials are elected. We must recognize and cultivate the "kingly anointing," even when these future leaders are yet children. When I speak of the kingly anointing, I am speaking of the principle of godly rule. Elected leaders must know how to govern with justice and pass laws with integrity. A president or governor or chief of police cannot think of himself or herself as a king, but he or she must rule with the humility, character and wisdom of Christ the King (see Luke 22:25–26).

The Gift of Democracy

Only in recent times has mankind been given a wonderful gift from God: democracy. For approximately 5,700 years the entire world order was ruled by kings and tribal chiefs (except for a partial democracy experienced briefly in Athens). Even today, nearly half the world does not elect its government leaders.

With democracy, we do not have to wait for a king or dictator to die, hoping that his heir will be more righteous. In America, every two, four and six years we are given the opportunity to pray and decide who shall guide our cities, states and nation. This means that we can choose godly leaders to guide us. Of course, no one is perfect. We will always struggle with the apparent imperfections of any candidate; we will never stop needing the priestly role of intercession to redeem our leaders' errors. But in democracies, we have the opportunity to realize the anointing of Christ in governmental systems. It is a tremendous gift from God!

Am I saying that democracy is the same as heaven? No, absolutely not! Not until Jesus returns will we realize the fullness of God's Kingdom. Remember, we said that our goal is not to see the Church become political but to see the political realm become spiritual, where the integrity, wisdom and justice of Christ—the kingly anointing of the Messiah Himself—manifest in godly leadership.

I have actually heard people say, "The Lord will decide who is elected. I'm not voting."

Excuse me, but in democracies God chooses to work through the voting system. We will always have to trust the

Lord no matter who is elected, and we should pray that He "stirs up" the spirits of godly people to vote, but He will not override the mechanics of our democratic nation. We must choose our officials with prayer and principled wisdom. We must also encourage others and work to see godly leaders positioned in government; and where godliness does not exist, we must pray for leaders, that they might come to Christ.

How do we discern among candidates which individual is capable of receiving Christ's anointing for government? First, we must look beyond an individual's debating skills and ask, "Does this man or woman bow to Christ as ruler?" You see, to that leader, Jesus must be revealed as the King of kings. Not until a person genuinely bows before Christ is he or she fit to rise and lead the people.

In every election in which you have the privilege of voting, support the individual who, as best as you can tell, is most open to the anointing of Christ the King. And remember, God calls us to pray for our leaders—those we voted for and those we did not—with faith and mercy, trusting in God's goodness.

Lord, my faith is in You, not man. Yet I know You have chosen a people through whom You desire to reveal Yourself. Grant us Christlike leaders in our society. Raise up godly statesmen and -women to represent You. In Jesus' name, Amen.

23

When America Blesses God

For the next couple of chapters, I will focus on my nation, America. And to connect to where we are going, I need to remind us of where we have been. Forgive my review of the past, but September 11, 2001, was a day that affected everyone in the United States. Like the attack on Pearl Harbor a half century earlier, it forced us to enter a reality that was terrifying and transforming. As a nation, we entered the war mode.

As a national leader and intercessor for America, I took the 9/11 attack very personally. Like everyone else, I was emotionally stunned by the sudden, massive devastation; yes, fear of further attacks flooded my mind. The impact of this attack sunk deep into my spirit. Somehow, these crazed Muslims had defied all the odds and accomplished destruction beyond the imaginable. Why did God allow this to happen?

My View of God's Wrath

On a myopic or personal scale, God's wrath and our sin are connected. If we sow to the flesh, we reap corruption (see Galatians 6:8). This level of wrath occurs because it is a principle integrated into all our lives—it is the consequence of sin. But this level is not a deliberate act of divine wrath in the sense that the Most High stands up and acts. For the most part, sin carries its own punishment.

However, divine wrath also occurs on another level, where God interrupts the escalation of sin and then destroys it before it gets worse. When this premeditated wrath of God manifests, heaven sponsors a preliminary effort to remove and protect the righteous. God does not swallow up the innocent in the punishment of the wicked.

This topic really needs its own book, as many things are at play behind the scenes. Put simply, however, I do not believe the September 11 terrorist attacks were the venting of wrath from God, as some have taught. God is both good and just. Hebrews 2:2 warns that "every transgression and disobedience [receives] a just penalty." Obviously, for the innocent, burning to death in a building or on an airplane is not a just penalty; it is disproportionate or unjust.

I could quote over a hundred verses to prove my point concerning divine justice and mercy, but for time's sake, let's consider Abraham's intercession for Sodom. Knowing the divine nature, Abraham prayed, "Will You indeed sweep away the righteous with the wicked? . . . Far be it from You to do such a thing" (Genesis 18:23, 25). In fact, if the Lord had found just ten righteous men, He would have forgiven Sodom. As it was, the only righteous people living there were Lot and his family. When God's wrath fell on Sodom, the Lord actually sent angels to rescue Lot. The angels hurried Lot's family along to a place of refuge, saying something quite remarkable. One said, "Hurry, escape there, for I cannot do anything until you arrive there" (Genesis 19:22).

Do you see this? The angel said, "I cannot do anything"—he could not act until the righteous were removed from the unrighteous. Actually, Lot was not very righteous himself if you study his life. But God would not destroy him with the wicked. Repeatedly, the Bible affirms the character of God. In times of divine wrath, the Lord separates the righteous from the wicked (see Genesis 9; 19; 1 Thessalonians 5).

Remember, also, our Savior's words concerning the wheat and tares. He taught that the Father is careful and will actually delay deserved wrath if the administration of that wrath will destroy the lives of the "wheat." Instead, He says, "Allow both [the tares and wheat] to grow together until the harvest; and in the time of the harvest I will say to the reapers, 'First gather up the tares and bind them in bundles to burn them up; but gather the wheat into my barn'" (Matthew 13:30).

When God judges, He separates the wicked from among the righteous. Some have argued that 9/11 was God's punishment for America's immorality and lawlessness. I say, if the Lord's wrath is kindled against the crimes of pornographers, drug dealers and abortionists in America, why should the "Judge of all the earth" kill and terrorize innocent people while the truly guilty walk away free?

Until the day I die, my confession shall be that God is good. It is the devil who is evil—who has come to "steal and kill and destroy" (John 10:10). For those who think 9/11 was God's wrath against Babylon (see Revelation 17–18), let's also consider the promise of God that He would bless (prosper) those who blessed Israel. Frankly, in spite of occasional disagreements, no nation on earth, ever, has stood with Israel as has the United States. Although questions may arise concerning our failed political attempts to broker peace, the vast majority of Americans love and support Israel with prayers and donations, and the United States government

167

itself continues to supply vast resources that help support Israel's economic and military needs.

Additionally, America is the most generous of nations. By far, Americans supply the most food and medical supplies to the poor of the world. The Lord promised prosperity to those who remember the poor. So for many reasons, I do not think in any way that the attacks of September 11, 2001, were God's wrath against Babylon.

Why Did God Allow the Attacks?

So if 9/11 was not a result of God's wrath, why did God allow it? As I sought the Lord, the Holy Spirit led me to review America as it was in the late 1930s. During that time, much of the world was engaged in a violent and terrible war. By 1940 *millions* of people had already died. Axis powers had mercilessly overrun nation after nation as they pursued their goal of world domination. This was an extremely serious time on earth. Yet America, in spite of our strength and resources, was not involved. Instead of engaging in efforts to stop the carnage, our primary efforts were spent trying to preserve our neutrality.

The strike against the United States at Pearl Harbor broke the spell of neutrality and awoke fierce and courageous resolve in America. In spite of all that was wrong with America at the beginning of World War II, God used this nation to help keep the lamp of freedom burning.

Yet the Lord's primary concern was His goal of spreading the Gospel. Since the end of World War II, hundreds of millions have come into the Kingdom of God. This great harvest simply would not have happened had the Axis powers won the war. Indeed, if our enemies had won, they would have undoubtedly persecuted and smothered the spread of true

Christianity. Additionally, the Nazis would have sought the complete annihilation of the Jews.

Today, we have another enemy: militant Islam. It, too, seeks world domination. We in the West know little about this religion. While moderate Muslims denounce the use of terrorism, millions of extremists follow the "conversion by conquest" example of Islam's greatest leaders. These extremists consider themselves Islam's "true believers" and have called for a holy war against infidel nations. This conquer-and-convert means of spreading Islam has brought death and slavery to many in African nations. It has released terrorism in numerous countries and has brought untold suffering to innocent millions around the world—and it is spreading rapidly. Yet initially, we in America did precious little to restrain this enemy.

The terrorist acts of September 11 jarred us to look into the face of this demonically manipulated world of Islamic fundamentalism. God has allowed us to drink the cup of this vile terrorism in order to unite us with those who, in other countries, have suffered under its hellish oppression. Not only has the Lord awakened us, He is now empowering us to war against it on two fronts: militarily and spiritually through prayer. His goal is to use the United States and our allies to stop Islam's quest for world domination.

I do not wish to imply that every move our military makes is an act of God. No, mistakes have been made and will continue to be made. This is, in part, why we must continue to intercede.

Wake-Up Call?

Many have pointed out the cultural relevance of the date September 11 or the numbers "9-1-1." What does it mean? Many say that 9/11 was a "wake-up call." Perhaps for them.

169

However, I have never dialed 911 and asked if they would awaken me at a certain time. The numbers 911 are an emergency code that calls trained personnel to desperate situations. September 11 was an emergency call to stand against Islamic terrorism.

This reality is deeply written on my spirit. I do not understand all that is involved, but I do know this: Every day I intercede for America and pray that no further massive attacks will occur. God burdens me inwardly and reminds me daily to pray for America's protection. I am urging you to do the same. Ask God to forgive America (or your nation if you are not American). Acknowledge our national sins to God in an act of identificational repentance, as did Daniel (see Daniel 9).

The war against us is serious. We must not allow lethargy or the fact that these wars seem like "old news" to deceive us into thinking that this war is over. We still must remain vigilant in prayer, for terrorists can use any multitude of ways to destroy our society. We must be guarded against biological and chemical warfare as well. There is no way any government could prevent such attacks with 100 percent accuracy. But God can ferret out these radicals and expose their plans.

This means that we must pray! It is time to war for the destiny of God for the nations. Stand in prayer for America, for Israel and for the Islamic peoples everywhere. Our war is not against flesh and blood, but against the spirits that are ruling and oppressing millions. Remember, it was after World War II that America made "In God We Trust" its national motto. Our nation learned to trust God during the terrible danger of WWII. God can preserve and protect us again.

When will our war be over? We will know we are close to victory when the Holy Spirit has transformed our culture— when with repentant yet thankful hearts, we turn fully to the

Almighty. Yes, our breakthrough will be close not only when people again say, "God bless America," but when America looks heavenward and blesses God.

Master, may my voice be another that rises from our land and blesses You! As one of Your representatives here on earth, I bless You. You are my great King. To You I pledge my undying allegiance. May all the nations bless You, Lord Jesus. In Your name, Amen.

24

The Lord of Armies

This book is called *This Day We Fight!* for a reason. Our nation has been under spiritual and physical attack. God has called His Church to step up, grow up, take up the sword of the Spirit and fight for the future. Beloved, we can see our nation turned away from sin and aggressively turned toward heaven. It is happening even as we speak, but we are not there yet. We will have to war.

It is no secret that today America is the most influential nation in the world. Yet consider how God could use our land if Hollywood experienced a revival and our government became a model of integrity and justice. Let's not doubt.

In 1990 the condition of America was cause for alarm. Our inner cities were in chaos; violence and injustice were spreading and seemingly unstoppable. Yet in the early 1990s, the prayer movement in America also started in earnest. At the same time, reconciliation and unity in the Body of Christ increased dramatically. Instead of lawlessness increasing, as many feared, crime actually began to decrease and continued to decrease for the next fifteen years. The prayer movement made great headway in changing the fabric of American culture.

However, in recent years the enemy has counterattacked, and his first line of attack was to quietly use a variety of means to pacify the prayer movement. Many Christians stopped believing that God was going to do something great; others became entangled in sin and other problems; still others, due to delays, became more focused on worldly objectives. The overall effect across the board was that prayer decreased in America.

Okay, round one is over—now it is time for round two. God is calling us back to vision and prayer. It is time to reload! It is time to pick up the sword of the Holy Spirit and join the ranks of the overcoming Church. It is time to resist that cloud of oppression and pray.

We are at the end of this book, but we are also at a new beginning in our war against evil. The Church in America is throwing off indifference and apathy and rising, at long last, to her feet. I urge you to field godly candidates for upcoming elections. I pray that if your church has no prayer group, you will be the person who starts one. I ask that if your neighborhood has no intercessors gathering together or your school is without united prayer warriors, you stand in the gap until God brings people who will stand with you.

I hope these pages have helped you find a new zeal and fresh anointing to war on behalf of righteousness. Whether we are speaking in reference to our own souls, our families, our cities or our nations, I believe that if we persevere, we have great days ahead.

I know some still say, "I don't get it. I don't understand this warfare, this battle mindset. I just don't see it in the Lord or the Scriptures."

I have saved this chapter for last because, in many ways, it is the most important. The enemy has been far too successful in blinding people's eyes both to the reality of who Christ is in His righteous wars against evil and also to the authority we have to represent Christ on earth. Many nominal Christians think of God as a combination of the chubby "Happiness Buddha" and a kindly Santa Claus. Nothing could be further from the truth. I know we are not supposed to be fearful, but an encounter with the living God or His angels is a terrifying experience. Note that I did not say *bad* but *terrifying*. God is not trying to scare us; it just happens. In the Bible, whenever a person saw the Lord or an angel—or even a glimpse of God's power—that individual instinctively passed out.

How many times in the Scriptures do we read of the Lord telling His servants, "Do not be afraid"? If you look at the context of these words, it is often just after one of His servants has seen Him and, in response, has fainted. The phrase that describes the typical human reaction to an experience with the real God is not that a person "felt goose bumps," but that he was "like a dead man." God is great. He is a mighty warrior. And He is on our side to lead us into victory.

The Lord and His Army

The enemy has been clever. He has been able to obscure in some fashion one of the greatest revelations of the Lord in the Bible. It is an aspect of the divine nature that is revealed in the compound names of God. Some familiar examples of these unique names are *Yahweh-Nissi* ("the Lord My Banner") or *Yahweh-Jirah* ("the Lord My Provider") or *Yahweh-Rapha* ("the Lord My Healer"). In revealing Himself via these names—on about thirty different occasions in the Bible—the Lord unites His eternal nature to the human need of His servants.

Yet one name stands apart from these thirty references. It occurs approximately two hundred ninety times in the Bible—nearly ten times the sum of all other revelations! Additionally, the context of literally hundreds of other Scriptures includes the meaning of this awesome revelation of God. What is that name? Let me introduce you to *Yahweh-Sabaoth*, "the Lord of Hosts." From the sheer number of references alone, we see that "the Lord of Hosts" (or the God of Armies) is the revelation of the Most High most frequently demonstrated to mankind in the Bible.

When we talk about fighting for our personal transformation or warring for our families, cities and nations, it is the Lord of Hosts we want to follow into battle. It was the Lord of Hosts who met Joshua on the plains of Jericho (see Joshua 5:14), and it was the God of Armies who led David into battle against the Philistines (see 1 Samuel 17:45).

If we are to succeed in our warfare, we need to see the Lord as the great Commander that He is, for it is the Commander of heaven's armies whom we follow. He is the Master of the universe, Lord of powers, both on earth and in heaven, "and the armies which are in heaven . . . [are] following Him" (Revelation 19:14).

Yet the enemy has seeded false images of these angelic armies into our thought-life to weaken our understanding of the power and might of God. Consider how every winter, millions pull out the Christmas decorations, take out the treetop angel, position it and plug it in. A beautiful white, blonde woman with wings and a long dress lights up, and the tree is complete. And without realizing it, we have sown what is likely a false image of an angel into our minds and the minds of our children.

Let me concede that it is possible angels have appeared to Christians in a feminine, comforting form on special occasions,

175

but there are no references to feminine angels in the Bible. Angels in the Bible are always depicted in a masculine form, even with masculine names, in warring postures or on special missions indicative of wartime. They appear as symbols of strength to help us. (The winged women in Zechariah 5 are not angels, but are actually symbols of wickedness.)

Simply, angels are fierce warriors of righteousness. They are clothed in light and mighty in battle. I am not sure what that winged woman on top of the Christmas tree represents, but it is not a biblical angel.

Nor are angels depicted biblically like little Gerber babies with wings, part of an Italian fresco and as harmless as they are cute. The cupid form of an angel originated in ancient Greece, where the cupid was known as Eros, the young son of Aphrodite, the goddess of love and beauty. This comes from Greek mythology. To the Romans he was Cupid, and his mother was Venus. Clearly, these images do not originate from the Scriptures.

Those were not "Gerber babies" that sang around the manger the holy night that Christ was born, either. Those were mighty, warring, heavenly beings singing in awe of the sacrifice of the great King.

Just once some Christmas, I would like to see a real angel show up on top of the tree just as I plug in the light—bam!—nuclear glory radiating, instantly frying the Christmas tree into a skeleton of smoldering sticks; everyone in the family slain spiritually, unable to move for hours under the weight of the angelic presence. A true "touched by an angel" episode and a Christmas to remember!

If I were in dreaded conflict with an evil principality or power, and I called on the Lord for help and a Gerber baby showed up, I would not feel much comfort. I do not care if the baby measured fifty feet tall—if he were wearing a diaper, I would not feel reassured. I want a real angel to show up, massive, terrifying, sword drawn, fire zooming out its eyes and hands, and with six wings. Real angels do not wear diapers. They are warriors in service to the Lord of Armies. They know how to fight.

Victor in Every Battle

Whatever your battle happens to be, the Lord of Armies is there for you. It was He who rescued you from the powers of darkness in the first place; it is this same Lord who comes now to anoint you for war and deliver you from the hand of the enemy. Indeed, the name *Jesus* by which we call our Redeemer is the transliteration of the Hebrew *Joshua*, the great general who led the armies of God into the Promised Land. *Jesus* means "Deliverer" as well as "Savior."

Consider David's revelation of the Lord of Hosts and pray this likewise for yourself:

> He delivered me from my strong enemy,
> And from those who hated me, for they were too
> mighty for me.
> They confronted me in the day of my calamity,
> But the LORD was my stay.
> He brought me forth also into a broad place;
> He rescued me, because He delighted in me.
>
> Psalm 18:17–19

Here is another promise:

> Fear not, for you will not be put to shame;
> And do not feel humiliated, for you will not be
> disgraced;
> But you will forget the shame of your youth,

177

> And the reproach of your widowhood you will re-
> member no more.
> For your husband is your Maker,
>   Whose name is the LORD of hosts;
>   And your Redeemer is the Holy One of Israel,
>   Who is called the God of all the earth.
>
> Isaiah 54:4–5

Or perhaps your battle right now is for your family, especially your children. They may be trapped in sin or addicted
to drugs. They may be seduced by some bad relationship or
an ongoing destructive habit. You have cried many tears for
them and feel as if your enemy is too strong, too mighty. You
want to give up. The Lord of Hosts has a promise for you.
Listen with faith as He speaks:

> "Can the prey be taken from the mighty man,
>   Or the captives of a tyrant be rescued?"
> Surely, thus says the LORD,
>   "Even the captives of the mighty man will be
>   taken away,
>   And the prey of the tyrant will be rescued;
>   For I will contend with the one who contends with
>   you,
>   And I will save your sons."
>
> Isaiah 49:24–25

Maybe your battle is for your city or nation. Again, we
must see the Lord as He is, a great warrior. If He is a fighter,
then you can expect He will impart His fight to you as well.
Here is His promise:

> The LORD will go forth like a warrior,
> He will arouse His zeal like a man of war.
> He will utter a shout, yes, He will raise a war cry.
> He will prevail against His enemies.
>
> Isaiah 42:13

Maybe you are praying for peace for Israel. Consider these words from the Lord of Hosts:

> In that day there will be a highway from Egypt to Assyria, and the Assyrians will come into Egypt and the Egyptians into Assyria, and the Egyptians will worship with the Assyrians.
>
> In that day Israel will be the third party with Egypt and Assyria, a blessing in the midst of the earth, whom the LORD of hosts has blessed, saying, "Blessed is Egypt My people, and Assyria the work of My hands, and Israel My inheritance."
>
> Isaiah 19:23–25

> Like flying birds so the LORD of hosts will protect
> Jerusalem.
> He will protect and deliver it;
> He will pass over and rescue it.
>
> Isaiah 31:5

Whatever your battleground, remember it is the Lord of Armies whom you follow and the Lord of Armies who fights for you. A great way to begin each day or to begin a prayer time or your Sunday service is by proclaiming the last half of Psalm 24:

> Lift up your heads, O gates,
>   And be lifted up, O ancient doors,
>   That the King of glory may come in!
> Who is the King of glory?
>   The LORD strong and mighty,
>   The LORD mighty in battle.
> Lift up your heads, O gates,
>   And lift them up, O ancient doors,
>   That the King of glory may come in!
> Who is this King of glory?
>   The LORD of hosts,
>   He is the King of glory.
>
> Psalm 24:7–10

Make room in your consciousness for the "Lord strong and mighty" to join you. He is the "Lord mighty in battle." Speak to the barriers and closed gates inhibiting your progress, that they may be lifted up "that the King of glory may come in!"

This unveiling of the Son of God as the Lord of Hosts is the most abundant revelation of His divine nature in the Bible. You should expect to know Him as a mighty, warring King. Ask God to reveal Himself to you as the Lord of Armies. It is a revelation that transforms a believer's wimpy old nature into a street fighter for Jesus.

Finally, let's consider the promise of God to His saints at the end of the age. Let's pray that we, too, will see heaven opened and behold realities as they are known from God's view.

> And I saw heaven opened, and behold, a white horse, and He who sat on it is called Faithful and True, and in righteousness He judges and wages war.
>
> His eyes are a flame of fire, and on His head are many diadems; and He has a name written on Him which no one knows except Himself.
>
> He is clothed with a robe dipped in blood, and His name is called The Word of God.
>
> And the armies which are in heaven, clothed in fine linen, white and clean, were following Him on white horses.
>
> From His mouth comes a sharp sword, so that with it He may strike down the nations, and He will rule them with a rod of iron; and He treads the wine press of the fierce wrath of God, the Almighty.
>
> And on His robe and on His thigh He has a name written, "KING OF KINGS, AND LORD OF LORDS."
>
> Revelation 19:11–16

Lord, my God, I sink my teeth into the truth of this message. You are my Commander. I see now that this world is a war zone and that You are engaged in the liberation of Satan's captives. Lead me, O Lord of Hosts! Train me for warfare, to fight and win the battles of the Lord! In Jesus' name, Amen.

Afterword

It was said of Winston Churchill that he "mobilized the English language and sent it into battle." I thank God for my friend Francis Frangipane, a true intercessor for America with a life of prayer I desire to emulate. When I read his book *This Day We Fight!*, the words awakened in me the primordial cry of a warrior, and I wanted to leap into Jehu's chariot and shout, "How can there be any peace as long as the witchcraft and harlotries of Jezebel are in the land?" (see 2 Kings 9:22).

Brothers and sisters, I know very few men like Francis who bear the image of Christ in kindness, forgiveness and reconciliation. Francis carries a towel on the earth. But, having heard about his experience of warring against the spirit of Jezebel, I know he also carries a sword in the heavens. Oh, the challenge of being like Jesus in our day—to love extravagantly and to war in prayer intensively. I want to be "a man of steel and velvet" such as Aubrey Andelin describes in his book by that same name (Pacific Press, 2006).

"Peace, peace" is the modern American mantra. This same spirit of false peace and passivity has neutralized much of the

Church in America, and many have wandered from the worship of the God who commands men everywhere to repent, the God who will judge the living and the dead, and whose Kingdom administration is built on fixed moral absolutes. Many have adopted the politics of neutrality and opted for peaceful coexistence and compromise with lifestyles and ideologies that directly counter God's Word and will ultimately destroy a nation. Our unwillingness to mobilize spiritual war over our own souls and our society has created a vacuum. Successive waves of evil have rushed into this vacuum and permeated every area of culture: in family, education, law and even the Church.

Satan has mustered his unseen supernatural forces of darkness, who have opened a floodgate of evil through ideologies that undermine God's authority. These ideologies promote men and women into arenas of influence from which they can shape and form the culture according to their own deceitful plans. Satan has now established his control centers whereby he can effectively oppose God's purposes in this nation. It was into such a context that the great Dutch reformer Abraham Kuyper thundered his challenge, "When the principles that began to win the day run against your deepest convictions, then peace becomes sin and war becomes your calling."

It is into such an American context that *This Day We Fight!* has been shot like an arrow from the fully bent bow of Francis's intercessory experiences. And though I write mainly from an American perspective, Francis's aim reaches much farther. Worldwide, the Church is called to stand and fight.

Again, when I read the book, it was like a modern-day *Braveheart* shaking me out of my illusions of self-preservation and a paralysis of passivity. The book recommissioned me to the battle command God gave me ten years ago thr॰ dream in which I heard, "No one is targeting false ideol° with massive fasting and prayer." I saw that the issues of à tion, the homosexual agenda, the pornographic plague à the rising tide of Islam could be overcome only by a conten ing house of prayer, for the sources fueling these ideologie are nothing less than unseen supernatural principalities and powers and forces of darkness in the heavenly realm.

On a forty-day fast in 1996, some colleagues and I were given a dream of a Buddhist house of prayer on top of a Christian house of prayer, which it dominated. In the dream the Christian house of prayer did a reversal and began to dominate the Buddhist house of prayer. It was there that God gave me my life job description: "Raise up a house of prayer that contends with every other house."

Such language is not politically correct in our culture, but without the sounding of the battle cry, the Church will never rise out of her lethargy to contend for the place of actual, not assumed, spiritual authority over the powers that come against her. Paul shouts across the ages that "our struggle is not against flesh and blood" (Ephesians 6:12), and again that "the weapons of our warfare are not carnal but mighty in God for pulling down strongholds" (2 Corinthians 10:4, NKJV). Jesus spoke of the spiritual violence of an even stronger one attacking the strongman and taking his spoils (see Luke 11:22).

Brothers and sisters, in *Born for Battle* Arthur Matthews wrote, "We have confined our living and interest to earth and have ignored our responsibilities in the heavens" (Harold Shaw Publishers, 2000). Abortion will not end, the homosexual will not be freed, the homosexual agenda will roll over the land and an Islamic ideology will govern in America unless the Church radically shifts her paradigm from programs to

pra~ ~asting and confrontation with the opposing powers.
As ~ur Matthews also commented in his book, "Barriers
w ~t be moved by God's omnipotence until the Church
~the initiative and stands her ground in the heavenly
~s to engage the powers of evil that are directly the cause
~round level troubles, and resists them in the name of the
~or of Calvary."

As of this writing, a seven-story "abortion supercenter"
~ecializing in late-term abortions is arising in the middle
~f Latino and black neighborhoods in Houston. Pull back
the spiritual curtain behind that building and you will see a
demonic Goliath. Give me a Latino leader who will stand up
and challenge the status quo with the words "We don't want
your death camps coming to our neighborhoods," and then
will also challenge the spirit of death with a prayer assault
by mobilizing united massive fasting and prayer against it.
The movie *Bella* portrays beautifully the Latino family and
exalts adoption over abortion. Let the Latinos fight for the
children with a great movement of adoption.

In the fall of 2009, a ministry called Bound4LIFE targeted
this massive Planned Parenthood abortion clinic that looks
like a cash register. Bound4LIFE engaged in a 21-day fast at
the same time that a ministry called 40 Days for Life mobilized thousands to pray and fast in front of abortion clinics
across America.

During this time of fasting, a young woman named Abby
Johnson, the director of a Planned Parenthood abortion clinic
near Houston, had a profound encounter. While watching
the ultrasound of an abortion, she experienced something
of a self-described "flash" and realized she had just seen the
death of a living person. She knew she could no longer be
part of this horrifying procedure. She resigned from Planned
Parenthood, and now she prays in front of the very clinic she

directed. She has told her story to millions through the media. This is nothing less than a "prayeradigm" shift.

Prayer binds the enemy's powers and enables people to see what they could not see before. Saul had such an encounter while breathing threats and bearing the authority to kill and imprison Christians. Suddenly a bright light shone, and Jesus revealed Himself to this raging adversary. Paul was led to a street called Straight, where scales fell off his eyes when the Jewish believer Ananias prayed for him. Paul, the man once persecuting Jesus, was now preaching Jesus to the whole Jewish world. Certainly the saints of Jerusalem, fresh from the Sermon on the Mount teachings of Jesus, were praying for Saul, who was persecuting them. Prayer blew open a portal in the heavens, and the rest is history.

Today homosexual activists are seeking to rewrite the laws of society and marriage. With courts and legislators overruling the very definition of marriage as being between a man and a woman, can we not see the mustering of demonic spirits pulling the strings of the judicial puppets? The crisis has stirred the Church as never before to war in fasting and prayer to restrain the ideology and to pray for those who are now persecuting her.

How stunned I was to hear recently of a homosexual prostitute who had a dream in which he got converted to Jesus. He woke up born again and saved, and God did a miracle in transforming his same-sex desires. The man has since appeared on Christian television to carry the message "Out of the closet and into the light." Again, what a "prayeradigm" shift!

If the Church will pray, thousands of others could similarly encounter Jesus and be led to their own "street called Straight." Great prayer battles were initiated in California and Maine that I believe turned back the homosexual ideology at the voting booths. We cannot let our hands fall down.

We are warring for the souls of our nation, our children and our children's children.

We have only toyed with the power of prayer. Muslims have a prayer culture while Christians have a prayer meeting. How can we contend with the spiritual powers released by millions of Muslims bowing five times a day and declaring, "There is no God but Allah and Muhammad is his prophet"? We can change.

Friends, things are changing. God is radically shifting His Church to become a contending house of prayer, and the fruit of it are testimonies such as this: In a recent telephone prayer meeting with thousands on the line across America, an ex-Muslim man said, "I came to America to destroy it with cultural jihad, but your God was a consuming fire. He saved me and delivered me. Now I am crying out for my Muslim brothers and sisters in America." He went on to say that last year, 23,000 Muslims came to Christ in America.

Yes! The house of prayer is blowing holes through the Muslim veil. We ought to be less concerned about the presence of potential terrorist immigrants coming into our country and more concerned about their salvation. Our main interest must not be self-preservation. Christians can die better than Muslims. If we are not going to them with the Gospel, maybe God is now bringing them to us. Oh, let it be that the Church, with her power to bind and loose in the name of Jesus, will take on the powers of darkness that fuel Islamic jihad. Let it be that the Church, through a massive movement of fasting and prayer, will loose angelic encounters and dreams to Muslims all across America! This is a call to love the Muslim on the ground, and to war against the spirits in the heavens. We must find the war mode Francis talks about within these pages. We must move from the realm of the defensive into the realm of the offensive.

Prayer is proliferating all over America. Tens of thousands have gathered in fields and stadiums and arenas to fast and pray. Day and night, unceasing worship and prayer have been arising out of Kansas City for ten years straight. Houses of prayer established at the doorsteps of Harvard, the Castro district and the Supreme Court building are targeting with laser-beam authoritative proclamation the powers of darkness that have held sway over these seemingly impregnable fortresses of darkness. God is beginning to challenge the powers, and He is finding a Church who knows her authority and is once again gaining air supremacy.

Jesus' Word thunders across the ages: "I will build My church, and the gates of Hades shall not prevail against it" (Matthew 16:18, NKJV). Jesus mobilized the Hebrew language and sent it into war. Let us answer our Commander-in-Chief's call with the battle cry *This Day We Fight!* Let us become the Church on a hill.

—Lou Engle
Founder and director, The Call

Francis Frangipane and his wife, Denise, live near Cedar Rapids, Iowa, and have five grown children. He is the author of sixteen books, including *The Three Battlegrounds* and *Holiness, Truth and the Presence of God*, which together have sold over one million copies.

Pastor Frangipane is also the director of Advancing Church Ministries (ACM), through which he conducts conferences, seminars and other ministry outreaches. The Holy Spirit has used the Christ-centered teaching of Francis Frangipane to unite thousands of pastors from many backgrounds around the world.

Pastor Frangipane has one primary vision, and that is conformity to Christ. To facilitate that vision for others, he has developed In Christ's Image Training (ICIT), an online school that now includes students in more than seventy nations. The ICIT basic course offers two levels of training:

Level I: Certification offers four foundational tracks: Christlikeness, humility, prayer and unity. Completion time, six months.

Level II: Growing in Christ offers further online teaching by Pastor Frangipane and other national church leaders. Completion time, three months.

To find out more about ICIT courses and tuition, please visit www.inchristsimage.org or email us at training@inchristsimage.org.

For books or audio and video training resources from Francis Frangipane, please visit www.arrowbookstore.com, call toll-free (877) 363-6889 or write Arrow Publications, Inc., P.O. Box 10102, Cedar Rapids, IA 52410-0102.

More from Francis Frangipane!

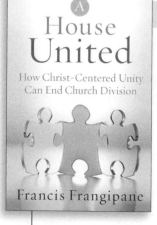

Bring Unity out of Division

Few works of the enemy are as destructive to the Body of Christ as a church split. As bitterness and grief seep into wounded hearts, congregations and pastors are left trying to find a sense of wholeness again.

Shining the bright light of Scripture into the shadows of division, beloved pastor Francis Frangipane exposes the demonic curse at work and explains what to do if your church is caught in turmoil. If you have experienced strain in the past or recognize a storm brewing in the present, A *House United* will guide you to restoration and peace while revealing biblical safeguards against future strife.

A House United by Francis Frangipane